Making Sure Your Everyday Decisions Move You Closer to God

RONNIE W. FLOYD

BROADMAN
& HOLMAN
PUBLISHERS

Nashville, Tennessee

Printed in the United States of America

4261-52
0-8054-6152-3

Dewey Decimal Classification: 248.4
Subject Heading:
DECISION MAKING // CHRISTIAN LIFE
Library of Congress Card Catalog Number: 94-10245

Scripture quotations are from the *New American Standard Bible,* © the Lockman Foundation, 1960, 1962, 1963, 1968, 1971, 1972, 1973, 1975, 1977; used by permission.

Library of Congress Cataloging-in-Publication Data
Floyd, Ronnie W., 1955–
  Choices : making sure your everyday decisions
  move you closer to God / by Ronnie W. Floyd
    p.   cm.
  ISBN 0-8054-6152-3
  1. Conduct of life. 2. Decision-making—Religious aspects—
Christianity. 3. Choice (Psychology)—Religious aspects—
  Christianity. I. Title.
BJ1581.2.F57   1994
248.4—dc20   94-10245
                                                         CIP

I would like to dedicate this book to my boys, Josh and Nicholas, who are everything to me and whom I love so much. In your lives, may you make the right choices which will lead you to experience God's power, so that your generation may know the power of Jesus Christ.

Contents

Acknowledgments

This book came into being out of a passion for my boys to grow up making the right choices in their lives. Since Jeana and I have been so blessed with two sons, Josh and Nicholas, our daily prayer for them is to be all God wants them to be.

Thanks need to be expressed to Jeana, Josh, and Nicholas for the sacrifices they made while I was writing this book and for sharing me with the precious people who will read it. I pray that our family will live out the principles contained in these pages.

I also want to thank Barbara Freeman, my administrative assistant, for all the help she provided. Countless hours were spent typing the manuscript and listening to my ideas. Thank you, Barbara, for all your assistance with this project. I also want to thank Dollie Havens, a friend and an encourager, who provided me with valuable suggestions concerning the manuscript.

I want to thank Chuck Wilson, Mike Hyatt, and Jimmy Draper for all they have done to assist me with this project. I am grateful for their trust and appreciate their journey to continually build a world-class publishing house.

In addition, I would like to acknowledge each person who will take time to read this book and implement its principles in his or her life. When you chose to read this book, you made a good choice. Whenever you put into practice the principles that will lead you to God's power, you will make great choices resulting in spiritual power, real success, and meaningful relationships.

Finally, I humbly acknowledge the power of the Holy Spirit to provide me with physical strength and spiritual energy to complete this book. Without His wonderful presence and leadership, this book never would have come into being. Thank You precious Holy Spirit.

❧

PART ONE

Choices

THE HIGH POWER OF CHOICE

THE POWER OF A RIGHT CHOICE

O N E

The High Power of Choice

Betsie and Corrie followed the guide through the door that led to their new home. The dormitory was dark, but their noses told them the place was filthy. Somewhere plumbing had backed up, and the bedding was soiled and rancid. As their eyes adjusted to the gloom, they saw there were no individual beds, but great square piers—thinly layered with reeking straw—stacked so high and so crowded together that the two women had to fight back feelings of claustrophobia.

They crawled to their places to lie down and try to sleep despite the nausea that swept over them. Suddenly, Corrie felt tiny, sharp stabs of pain cover her legs. She bolted upright, striking her head on the bunk above as she did. "Fleas!" she cried. "This place is swarming with them! How can we live in a place like this?"

Betsie thought for a moment and replied, "He's given us the answer . . . in the Bible this morning. Where was it?"

Corrie fumbled for the hidden Bible and made sure no guard was in sight. "It was in 1 Thessalonians," she said. "Here it is: 'Comfort the frightened, help the weak, be patient with everyone. See that none of you repays evil for evil, but always seek to do good to one another and to all.'" The words seemed to them to have been written expressly for Ravensbruck, the German concentration camp to which they had just been hauled like animals for hiding Jews in their homeland of Holland.

"Go on," said Betsie. "That wasn't all."

"Oh yes," Corrie added, "'Rejoice always, pray constantly, give thanks in all circumstances—'"

"That's it, Corrie! 'Give thanks in all circumstances!' That's what we can do!"

Together, these two sisters began to humbly give thanks for the Bible in their possession, for the lives God would allow them to touch because of their crowded conditions, and even for the fleas.

On that cold day in Ravensbruck, Betsie and Corrie ten Boom made a choice. They chose to give thanks for their situation and to find God's purpose in it rather than groan over their plight and seek an escape from it. This was hardly the first, and certainly not the last, time they had been faced with making a choice that would lead them to spiritual power. There was the pain they experienced from the brutality of prison guards. There were the humiliating experiences of being stripped of their clothing and sneered at by degenerate men. In spite of it all, Betsie and Corrie deliberately made choices that gave them spiritual power few people in this world comprehend. They chose to love their enemies rather than hate them; they chose to forgive their tormentors rather than be hostile toward them.

Perhaps one reason they could make such choices was because they had learned many years earlier the importance of making good choices. Corrie had learned as a young woman to love even when she was rejected. When Karel, the young man she had hoped to marry, introduced her to his fiancée, Corrie felt both surprise and heartbreak. But in the days that followed, she made a conscious choice. She chose to love Karel and his wife as God loved them and prayed for their happiness.

Years later, as German troops began to steal the peace and happiness from her village, Corrie already knew how to love her enemies and pray for them. She already knew how to choose to trust God's sovereignty and refuse to let fear direct her actions. Consequently, it was not a difficult decision for Corrie and her family to choose to hide Jews in their home, even though it meant risking their lives.[1]

We seldom see people making such brave and unselfish choices today. Few people experience the incredible power of choice as Corrie and Betsie ten Boom.

We might ignore the choices of these two women fifty years ago, thinking their circumstances were so unusual that their decisions have nothing to do with the reality of making decisions in our day. After all, times have changed and our culture is very different from World War II Europe. While the situations we encounter may be different, and not so dramatic, the choices we make are just as important if we are to experience spiritual power. And, yes, even in the midst of the confusion and pressures of our day, it is possible to make these right choices.

Making the Right Choice

Consider Charlie Ward, the Florida State University quarterback who received college football's highest honor, the Heisman Trophy. Without a doubt, many outstanding football players deserved this great honor. So what enabled the judges to single out Charlie Ward?

His statistics were certainly impressive—he completed 473 of 759 passes for 5,747 yards and 49 touchdowns. He played basketball for FSU after football season concluded. While Charlie's athletic ability and achievements are commendable, there are other reasons this young man is so admired and respected, both by his critics and his peers.

Charlie Ward has earned respect because he has learned the high power of choice. The choices he has made make him exceptional, not only as an athlete, but as a person with strong standards for his life.

"A young man like Charlie Ward is a leader not just because he can throw a football and dribble a basketball. He possesses intangible qualities that make others gravitate toward him. For Ward, those intangibles have been developed because of two basic reasons: Family and faith."[2]

Ward's basketball coach echoes this feeling when he speaks of how everyone respects Charlie, including coaches, teammates, managers, and fans.

Proper values are best learned in the home. Charlie learned to make right choices from the example set by his parents. They made church a vital part of their family life and taught their children the importance of being good citizens. Saturday nights were spent with all eight members of the family sitting at the table discussing how Jesus had blessed them the previous week.

Charlie learned the value of education and, in spite of his potential to succeed as a professional athlete, placed a priority on completing a degree in therapeutic recreation. By selecting this field of study, Charlie equipped himself to help people who have had severe head and brain injuries.

As a young person, Charlie learned the importance of making moral choices and has avoided the "party" lifestyle so readily available to him as a popular college athlete. In speaking about moral dangers, Charlie says, "You have to stick to what you believe in. You have to have a strong will and a faith in the Lord that He will guide you in the right direction. If you have that, regardless of what happens, He won't let you fall."[3] Charlie is quick to let everyone know that God is important in his life.

In spite of Charlie's great success as an athlete, he has maintained an attitude of humility. Few athletes with his record would be so self-sacrificing. During the 1993–94 season Charlie reached out to an incoming freshman named Warrick Dunn and asked him to be his roommate. Charlie knew Warrick was going through a difficult time due to the recent death of his mother. Ward quickly became like a big brother to Dunn.

Most people make choices daily without giving much thought to them.

Obviously, there are many reasons why Charlie Ward deserved the Heisman Trophy. He stands as a model of the high power of choice because he has demonstrated the desire to make choices that lead to real power—spiritual power—to influence others in a positive way.

Even though most people make choices daily without giving much thought to them, we as Christians are called to the high power of choice. The high power of choice is a right response to the options we are given every day. The high power of choice leads to spiritual power, real personal success, and meaningful relationships in life. As we seek to learn about the high power of choice, we need to begin our journey by understanding . . .

The Difference Between Liberty and Freedom

The average American becomes outraged at the thought of someone stealing their freedom. Legal suits, conflict among persons, and many battles and wars have been fought to preserve the freedom of a person, a group, or even a country. In our own country, we are committed to remaining "the land of the free."

The paradox of freedom is that while we become outraged at another for attempting to steal our freedom, many of us give our freedom away every day. The most unhappy people I know are those who shout the loudest about "being free" or "having their rights," yet are victims of their own choices. They do not understand the high power of choice.

In their blindness, their choices lead them not to freedom, but to enslavement to sin. The drug user, the child abuser, the homosexual, the pornography addict, or even we who may not be involved in such obvious sin, choose bondage every time we choose to sin rather than to exercise the high power of choice. When any of us becomes a victim of our choices, we are enslaved to sin. The result is unhappiness.

A Fresh Look at Liberty and Freedom

It may seem presumptuous to redefine the words *liberty* and *freedom*. However, for the sake of understanding the very heart of this book, it is important to clarify their meanings.

Liberty permits choice; however, genuine freedom is the power to make the right choice from the existing options. Every person has the liberty to do what he wants within the structure of the law of the land without judicial complications. Yet most of the choices we make, even though within the law, can still be wrong choices for us spiritually, socially, and personally.

Corrie and Betsie ten Boom had liberty taken from them. Their imprisonment was as treacherous as weeks of solitary confinement and as brutal as the German concentration camp. Yet they were always free to love and forgive. The result was spiritual power.

Charlie Ward had the liberty to make choices for the sake of popularity or pleasure or comfort. Instead, he made a higher choice that resulted in his freedom from enslavement to sin. His choices resulted in spiritual power. These examples should motivate us to make the right choices so we can experience spiritual power rather than enslavement to poor choices.

A Heisman Look Back

Again, Charlie Ward's life illustrates this understanding of liberty and freedom. He practices the high power of choice even though he may not be aware of this terminology. The result of his choices is personal fulfillment and success.

In his days at Florida State University, Charlie had the liberty to choose his personal, social, and athletic lifestyle. Charlie had the liberty to be arrogant because he was named the greatest collegiate athlete in 1993. He had the liberty to be boastful because he was starting quarterback for the 1993 national championship team. He had the liberty to choose the "party lifestyle" of a university campus, but he chose a private and controlled lifestyle. He even had the liberty to live so privately that his life rarely intersected with others. Instead, he chose to encourage and challenge others with a strong quiet leadership style.

The model he has presented during his university life as a nationally acclaimed athlete illustrates the high power of choice. Yes, he had the liberty to choose, but greater than that, he exercised the high power of choice by rightly responding to the various options given to him. His family and faith instilled in him a passion to make right choices which spiritually empower his life, rather than victimize his life through their consequences.

One of the ways we become victims of our choices is because of a problem I identify as . . .

A Deceived Mentality

The abortion issue has become one of the hottest controversies of our day. Conservative estimates are that at least thirty million abortions have taken place in America since 1973, almost one-half of the population of our baby boomer generation in our country.

Who knows whether one of these infants would have grown up to give society the gift of a cure for cancer or Aids. One of these infants might have been chosen by God as a major world leader of great influence for the good of all. More importantly, one may have been God's special, anointed prophet used to bring world revival. We will never know the extent of what the world has lost because these precious lives were taken. And just think, this loss to the world was intentional, and all done in the name of choice.

The abortion issue illustrates this deceived mentality. People often proclaim themselves pro-choice, meaning they favor the legal right for mothers to choose whether they want to have their babies. These same people often go one step further saying they are also pro-life, explaining that they do not personally believe in abortion or practice it, but do believe everyone should have the right to choose. Slick-tongued politicians and powerbrokers make this argument sound right to the American public. However, I believe it indicates a deceived mentality. We are deceived when we make choices that will result in others being hurt, injured, or murdered.

Women in our society have the liberty to choose abortion; however, if they make that choice, they become victims of their choice. They will not experience freedom because freedom only comes to those who have the power to discern the right choice from the various options available. The right choice is always congruent with the heart of God revealed in His Word. The killing of the unborn is never justified in the Bible. Those who become victims of this wrong choice often experience personal guilt and remorse the rest of their lives.

Why does this occur? What is the problem? A deceived mentality exists in our society. This mentality also operates in many other difficulties, such as abuse in the family, cheating the Internal Revenue Service at tax time, mistreating employees or employers, disrespect for authority of any kind, exposure to violence and sensuality, double-mindedness toward others, violation of personal integrity, being at church on Sunday but living a reckless, un-Christlike life the other days of the week, and in other ways too numerous to mention.

Why does this deceived mentality exist? Let me suggest three reasons it is so prevalent.

Rationalism

Rationalism is the belief that human reason is the source of knowledge. Rationalism does not consider God or what He says in His Word, but permits each person to decide what is right in his own eyes. Rationalism ruins lives, destroys families, creats an unsafe society, and choks the spiritual life out of our nation.

Rationalism has existed since the Garden of Eden. When God gave Adam and Eve the right to choose, instead of making the right choice, they rationalized. They immediately became victims of their sinful choice. Adam and Eve had the freedom to choose, but they gave it away when they made the wrong choice. They traded personal freedom for personal enslavement.

Throughout American society, people daily rationalize wrong choices. Their human reasoning or rationalization excuses all forms of abuse, the problems of pornography, violence, self-gratification, abortion, homosexuality, all forms of evil, carnality in the lives of Christians, and spiritual lethargy in the church. This tide will not be turned until people are empowered by God to make right choices from the options available.

This deceived mentality does not exist solely because of rationalism, but also because of . . .

Irresponsibility

A twisted view of liberty has existed for so long in our society that vast numbers of people do not sense responsibility for the choices they make. In this excused age in which we live, too many people mentally exempt themselves from responsibility for the choices they make. This causes so many problems in our world.

Too many people mentally exempt themselves from responsibility for the choices they make.

A great tragedy in today's American culture is the lack of responsibility demonstrated through breaking marriage vows. It is quite common, not only in the secular world, but also within the church, for men who have been married a number of years to announce to their spouses, "It is over." After sharing their lives and their children for years, extramarital affairs begin and suddenly five, ten, twenty or more years are tossed away.

The perplexing thing about this is the irresponsibility for these actions by those who walk away. In their minds, with their deceived mentality, they do not feel responsible to their spouses, their children, and many times, to God. In fact, the deceit is so powerful, they often feel entitled to make such a choice in the name of self-identity; in reality, it is only human selfishness.

Our society may permit this in the name of liberty, but these people will not be free personally. The high power of choice requires us to make responsible choices that lead us to spiritual vitality, not spiritual callousness. This deceived mentality is fueled by selfish rationalism and justified by irresponsibility, and it is evident to a greater degree than ever before because of . . .

Unaccountability

A deceived mentality operates at optimum levels in our society because of a lack of accountability. From the church house to the state house to the White House, accountability is needed for the protection of individuals and the good of society. No one is too big, too important, or too powerful to be accountable to other people and to God.

Whether in family, business, church, or pleasure, each of us needs to be accountable to someone. Our accountability to others can help shield us from this deceived mentality which produces rationalism and irresponsibility.

Each of us needs as a permanent backdrop for our minds and hearts the reality that we are accountable to God. One day we will stand before Him, and as Romans 14:12 reminds us, "So then each one of us shall give account of himself to God."

This means we will give a word-by-word account of our lives to God. The pastors and preachers of this land must always have the courage to remind people they are accountable to God. This message may not be popular, but it is necessary to preserve us from the deceived mentality of our society.

Since this deceived mentality robs us of the high power of choice by excusing our choices in the name of liberty, we become victims of our wrong choices. Therefore, it is to our advantage spiritually and practically to evaluate what happens when we make poor choices. Consider now . . .

The Downside of a Poor Choice

When a person owns stock in a company, he often is paid dividends. These dividends are determined by the profit made in a given period of time. Therefore, each stockholder receives something for his investment in the company. The choices the company makes determine the amount of dividends paid to the stockholder.

When we make choices, we are not stockholders but stakeholders. Something is at stake in the choices each of us makes. A positive choice generates spiritual strength and power, but a negative choice drains life of spiritual strength and power.

When we buy into this philosophy of life, we become deceived and begin to make poor choices because we place emphasis on "what seems to be good for me" rather than on "what God wants in my life." As a result, we begin to experience the downside of our poor choices.

From 2 Samuel 11 we learn that King David stayed in Jerusalem as other kings were going out to battle. He chose not to do what a king was supposed to do. He made a poor choice. He was negligent in his responsibilities, another poor choice.

Later, David was walking on his roof because he could not sleep, and he saw a beautiful woman, Bathsheba, bathing. As her king, he sent for her and had sexual relations with her. Through this encounter, a married woman became pregnant with David's child. David was so drawn to Bathsheba that he had her husband,

Uriah, sent to the front lines of battle to insure his death. Subsequently, David took Bathsheba as his wife. Their baby died seven days after it was born.

David demonstrated nothing of the high power of choice. His initial choice of negligence became dreadfully compounded by lust, self-gratification, and ultimately, murder. It seems that the devil "greased the slide" for a quick path to destruction.

David became a victim of his choices; the consequence of these choices was spiritual bondage because he did not exercise the spiritual power to make the right choice—God's choice! He gave away his freedom by doing what he wanted to do rather than choosing what he should have done. He experienced personally the downside of a poor choice. Through this biblical story, consider three proofs of the downsides of poor choices. These were true for David, and they are true for every other person who makes poor choices.

Limited Spiritual Power

David's choices, so often detrimental to his life, limited his spiritual power. It is obvious from 2 Samuel 12 that David sinned greatly against the Lord. As the prophet Nathan rebuked him, David finally repented of his sinful choices; but his choices had already brought him much grief and sorrow. The greatest tragedy of these poor choices was that they robbed him of spiritual power. Once the downward slide began, his limited spiritual power rendered him helpless to stop the slide. He became completely deceived.

> One of the really motivating reasons for practicing the high power of choice is spiritual power.

One of the really motivating reasons for practicing the high power of choice is spiritual power. A right choice expands spiritual power. A poor choice retards spiritual power. Our challenge is not to choose what we want to do, but to have the power to make the right choice—God's choice.

Counterfeit Success

Another downside of a poor choice is counterfeit success. Once we are deceived, we buy into a counterfeit value system and its definition of success.

In spite of David's poor choices, he was still king. He continued to enjoy the privileges of being king. He had the sensual pleasure of adultery and the challenge of covering it up. However, once Bathsheba became pregnant, the situation became very complicated. Was David a successful person? By the standards of a valueless world system—yes! But his success was counterfeit. In fact, not until David was rebuked by the prophet Nathan did he become aware of how powerfully he had been deceived. I imagine that when the scales of blindness fell from David's eyes, he probably asked himself, "Why am I doing this? This is not me nor what I stand for."

A poor choice will never lead to authentic success—success by God's standards. Only the high power of making the right choice leads to real success. I believe we must evaluate whether we are experiencing real success or counterfeit success.

I have heard that when people are trained to detect counterfeit money, they do not look at counterfeit bills. They are trained by studying the genuine articles. By learning what real money looks like, it becomes quite simple to detect its counterfeit.

We must always know what God and His Word say about real success so that when deception comes from Satan and this world's value system, we are readily able to identify that deception as counterfeit, wrong, and un-Christlike. This will enable us to experience the high power of choice which leads to spiritual power and success.

Disrupted Relationships

David's poor choices resulted in a life filled with tragedy and disrupted relationships. David's relationship with Uriah, his trusted soldier, ended with Uriah's death. His relationship with Nathan became strained until David repented of his sin. His relationship with his firstborn child ended when the baby died. David's life represents a a series of poor choices. Because of his choices, failure began to creep into David's life at the very height of his success. His personal goals began to dominate him, leading him to neglect his family. This was the first in a whole series of poor choices which, in turn, resulted in a promising life filled with tragedy.

Every decision we make affects others. We do not live in isolation; so, when we make poor choices, disrupted relationships result. This downside of poor choices breaks up friendships, destroys families, and creates an unstable society infested with crime and violence.

Making the right choices will give us spiritual power, genuine success, and a life full of meaningful relationships.

Yes, David had the liberty to do these things, but he gave his freedom away every time he made a poor choice. Misery must have been his close companion. His life needs to serve as a great warning for us. Even a "man after God's own heart" may make very poor choices. However, the interesting thing about David is that, in time, he always came back to God. His heart was right; but his choices were often poor.

The challenge for us is to have a right heart that prompts us to make right choices. This will save us from experiencing limited spiritual power, counterfeit success, and disrupted relationships. Conversely, making the right choices will give us spiritual power, genuine success, and a life full of meaningful relationships. Which of these do you desire?

The Dilemma Before Us

The high power of choice is a personal decision. It is not just a one-time choice, because it involves multiple decisions from multiple choices every day. No one can make our choices for us; we stand alone as we consider our options.

I love to go to Baskin-Robbins for ice cream. With thirty-one flavors to choose from, a person cannot go wrong unless he selects a flavor he does not like. Normally, I am a risktaker; but when I go to Baskin-Robbins I create a win-win situation for myself. I choose either chocolate or world-class chocolate ice cream. There is nothing wrong with the other flavors, but I like these two and I know choosing one or the other is the right choice for me.

Unfortunately, the choices we often have to make do not create win-win situations, but win-lose. If our choice is between God's way or our way, we make a win-lose decision. Therefore, our daily challenge is to make the right choice. We never can go wrong choosing God's way or God's Word.

Every day our lives are filled with choices as varied as a Baskin-Robbins menu. The only difference is that these choices are much more costly than a simple dip of ice cream.

The high power of choice calls us to make positive choices—God's choices! These choices cannot be made in the name of liberty; they must be made for the sake of freedom—freedom to do what we should do rather than what we want to do.

Liberty emphasizes the importance of the tangibles in life, the things we can see, hear, or feel. Freedom resides within an individual. Its concern is the power to make right choices, the kinds of choices that lead a person to live in peace with God and to know he or she has made the right choice.

In the words of #17, winner of the 1993 Heisman Trophy and quarterback of the 1993 national football champions, Charlie Ward, "You have to stick to what you believe in. You have to have a strong will and a faith in the Lord that He will guide you in the right direction."[4]

Charlie Ward understands the high power of choice.

There are few in the world who will ever receive the accolades of a Charlie Ward. Fewer still will face the extreme challenges of a concentration camp like Betsie and Corrie ten Boom did.

However, each of us can receive the blessings of God when we make right choices. We will experience this high power of choice when we make the right choice—God's choice—from the many options available everyday.

❧

TWO

The Power of a Right Choice

The five greatest choices you will ever make in your life, other than how you will respond to Jesus Christ, are:

How much education will I obtain?
Who will I marry?
If I marry, will I have children and if so, how many?
What will be my vocation in life?
Where will I live?

Each of these choices involves many options. A wrong choice in any one of these five areas may result in a life of failure. A right choice in any of these areas will empower you for living. There is power in making the right choice.

As a boy, I wanted to be a coach, preferably a football coach. I learned the game, studied the game, and was consumed with the game. Every now and then, when I learn of a young man being hired at a major university, I say to my wife, "That could have been me."

There is nothing wrong with wanting to be a coach; however, that was not the right choice for me. God wanted to use me in ministry rather than in athletics. One of the best blessings I have in the ministry is the opportunity to influence others in the coaching profession.

I am often asked, "How did you choose the ministry as your vocation?" I always quickly respond, "I did not choose the ministry. God chose it for me." I really believe God wants to help each person choose a vocation. In fact, let me share with you how God helped me to see what He wanted to do with my life.

My mother and father raised me in a Christian home. We attended church every time the doors were opened. When I was a young boy, I responded publicly to an invitation at the end of our worship service one Sunday because a good friend of mine made a decision to seek spiritual help. I was given a card to complete, congratulated by the pastor, and baptized shortly after being introduced to the church. No one ever explained to me my need to turn from sin and by faith receive Jesus Christ into my life. As a result, I began life as a church member without being a Christian. It frightens me to think how many people share a similar experience as mine.

Years later, our small church called a young man named Mike Shillings to be our pastor. He was only nineteen years of age. At the time, I was fifteen years old. I had never met a more vibrant, energetic, contagious Christian. It was not long after meeting him until I discovered I did not have the same kind of relationship to Jesus Christ that Mike did.

One Saturday evening while attending a youth fellowship led by this young pastor, I came to the full realization that I needed to turn from my sinful ways and trust Jesus Christ as my Savior. So, at the altar of that small church, I did just that and began to experience the power of a right choice.

Three months later, our church had a men's day. The pastor could not persuade any of the men to preach, so he asked me if I would be interested. I immediately accepted his challenge. God began that day preparing my heart to be in the ministry.

There were two preachers in our area of Texas who were preaching regularly in various churches. I would come home from school, do my homework, and go with friends to hear these men, intense and fiery motivational preachers of the gospel of Jesus Christ. As a sixteen-year-old boy, I felt those men were absolutely electric with the power of the Holy Spirit.

I began to feel the heavy burden of God's call, even though at the time, I was not sure what it was. While attending one of those local church meetings, I responded to the invitation for public decisions, asking one of those great men to pray for me because God was working in my life. I will never forget his prayer: "Lord, if you want Ronnie in the ministry, make him miserable until he surrenders to your call; if you are calling him and he will not surrender, kill him." That prayer would get the attention of any sixteen-year-old boy wanting one of his spiritual heroes to pray for him. It certainly got mine.

God answered that preacher's prayer. For days, I was miserable. Finally, in a Sunday morning service in my own church, I walked down the aisle, embraced my pastor, and shared with him God's call to me into the ministry to preach the gospel. God must have revealed my call to others in the church because so many told me they were not surprised.

Power immediately moved into my life because of that right choice. Many could not understand how I had made that decision and probably thought I would change my mind in the future. But they did not understand that God had called me to preach His Word. There was a higher power than mine drawing me into ministry. It was the Lord's power.

I am the one most amazed that God chose me to be one of His preaching servants. I am astounded at the opportunities God has brought to my life. While growing up in that small church, it was a good day if forty people attended. I used to think while driving around that small town how great it would be to one day pastor a church with two hundred people in attendance. To me, that was a big church.

God has blessed my life and ministry far beyond my expectations. These blessings have come for two reasons. First, I experience the grace of God being lived out in my life; I do not merit any of His blessing—they are gifts of grace. Second, I made a right choice about what I felt God wanted me to do in life.

> *Just as there are negative consequences in making a bad choice, there is spiritual power in making a right choice.*

My point is simple—power accompanies right choices. Just as there are negative consequences in making a bad choice, there is spiritual power in making a right choice. Always remember that a right choice is God's choice. How you answer the questions and decide between the options of life will determine whether you have spiritual power in your life.

The Ultimate Question

King David was wearing down as he advanced in years. In 1 Kings 1, we read about David naming his son Solomon to succeed him as king. In 1 Kings 2, the Bible records how David challenged Solomon before his death by saying,

> And keep the charge of the Lord your God, to walk in His ways, to keep His statutes, His commandments, His ordinances, and His testimonies, according to what is written in the law of Moses, that you may succeed in all that you do and wherever you turn, so that the Lord may carry out His promise which He spoke concerning me. (vv. 3–4)

Shortly after saying these words, King David died. Even though some may remember David for his poor choices, we need to remember that God called him a man after His own heart. David also made many right choices in his life. One of the greatest of these was passing on to his son a spiritual legacy.

So Solomon became king and began on the right path by making a great choice when asked the ultimate question by the Lord. In 1 Kings 3:5, the Bible says, "In Gibeon the Lord appeared to Solomon in a dream at night; and God said, 'Ask what you wish me to give you.'"

The question posed to Solomon is definitely an ultimate question. God told him he could have anything he wished. Solomon only had to name it and God would give it to him.

Even though Solomon's spiritual heritage was great, this must have been quite a challenge, considering his youthfulness and zeal. As Solomon remembered his father's heart for God, he may have also remembered some of his father's sinful choices. Therefore, how would he answer God's question? Would his human weakness or his desire to please God determine his choice? Would he experience the power of a right choice or the downside of a wrong choice?

Solomon was about to determine the level of spiritual power he wanted in his life. This question was of great magnitude, because the options from which he could choose were too great to even number. Therefore, consider with me . . .

The Ultimate Options

In the summer of 1993, my wife and I spent the evening at a wonderful hotel in Asheville, North Carolina. Located in the beautiful Smoky Mountains, the hotel takes full advantage of the scenery.

In the hotel was a restaurant known for its splendid, world-class seafood buffet. It was all beautifully prepared and elegantly presented. Where would I begin? How much could I eat? Should I try a little bit of everything? The choices were overwhelming.

As great as that seafood buffet was, its options were nothing in comparison to what Solomon had facing him. When God told him He would give him whatever he wished, Solomon faced the ultimate options of life. Solomon could have asked for a long life. He could have asked for all the world's riches. He could have asked for all his nation's enemies to be destroyed. He was guaranteed a fulfillment of his request by the Lord Himself. What more could anyone ask?

Our choices will convey our values and our spiritual relationship to God.

I do not believe any of us has ever been in this exact situation like Solomon. Yet we daily face multiple options with most decisions we make. At times we feel overwhelmed by so many options. Sometimes we wish right choices were clearly indicated and easy to make and at times we would welcome someone else making our choices for us.

In reality, each of us faces the ultimate options of life every day. Sometimes we have only a few options to choose from and at other times many. Our choices will convey our values and our spiritual relationship to God. We must be committed to making the right choices which will lead us to experience the power of God in our lives.

The Ultimate Choice

God must have been very pleased when Solomon's request reflected a solid, spiritual choice. In 1 Kings 3:7–10, we read of Solomon's answer to the Lord's question when he said,

"And now, O Lord my God, Thou has made Thy servant king in place of my father David, yet I am but a little child:

I do not know how to go out or come in. And Thy servant is in the midst of Thy people which Thou has chosen, a great people who cannot be numbered or counted for multitude. So give Thy servant an understanding heart to judge Thy people to discern between good and evil. For who is able to judge this great people of Thine?" And it was pleasing in the sight of the Lord that Solomon had asked this thing.

Solomon desired more than anything else in the world an understanding heart. This understanding heart is called wisdom. First Kings 4:29–30 records, "Now God gave Solomon wisdom and a very great discernment and breadth of mind, like the sand that is on the seashore. And Solomon's wisdom surpassed the wisdom of all the sons of the east and all the wisdom of Egypt."

God had told Solomon in the dream He would give him whatever he desired. These words from 1 Kings 4 verify that God granted Solomon's request. Just think, from all the choices he had, Solomon wanted wisdom. This warrants us to ask . . .

What Is Wisdom?

In the Old Testament, wisdom was the art or skill of living your life to fulfill God's desires for you. It excluded delusions, craftiness, shrewdness, and magic. In fact, Proverbs 2:6 verifies what was believed about wisdom. As it says, "For the Lord gives wisdom; from His mouth come knowledge and understanding."

The Bible instructs us that wisdom comes only from God. It has nothing to do with human reason or calculation; these are regarded as foolishness, the opposite of wisdom. Therefore, when a person makes his choices from a human perspective, he is practicing foolishness. Conversely, when a person makes his choices from God's perspective, he is practicing wisdom.

W. E. Vines' *Expository Dictionary of Biblical Words* defines *wisdom* as, "Knowledge and ability to make the right choices at the opportune time. The consistency of making the right choice is an indication of maturing and development."

This definition gives us the real impact of the kind of wisdom Solomon requested from God. He desired to make the right choices at the opportune time. He wanted to demonstrate consistency in making the right choices. This would be living proof that he was maturing and developing into the kind of king the Lord wanted him to be. He desired the power to make right choices.

Wisdom is seeing life the way God sees it and making the choices He wants us to make.

In the New Testament, wisdom refers to being prudent and sensible, and being practically and spiritually wise. In concluding His Sermon on the Mount, Jesus said, "Therefore, everyone who hears these words of Mine, and acts upon them, may be compared to a wise man, who built his house upon the rock" (Matt. 7:24).

Wisdom is seeing life the way God sees it and making the choices He wants us to make. When we operate our lives by this kind of wisdom, we are building our lives on a solid foundation which can withstand the winds of adversity and change.

Was Wisdom the Right Choice?

Of all the things for which Solomon could have asked, he asked for the best. He chose wisdom. Solomon could have chosen health, wealth, fulfilling relationships, or any other thing. However, he made the right choice—wisdom. Every leader, every Christian, every person needs wisdom. That is always the right choice for you and me, for it ensures spiritual power in our lives.

The Bible records God's interesting response to Solomon's desire for wisdom in 1 Kings 3:11–15:

> Because you have asked this thing and have not asked for yourself long life, nor have asked riches for yourself, nor have you asked for the life of your enemies, but have asked for yourself discernment to understand justice, behold, I have done according to your words. Behold, I have given you a

wise and discerning heart, so that there has been no one like you before you, nor shall one like you arise after you. And I have also given you what you have not asked, both riches and honor, so that there will not be any among the kings like you all your days. And if you walk in My ways, keeping My statutes and commandments, as your father David walked, then I will prolong your days.

The very thing Solomon asked for he received. The many things he could have asked for—things many of us might have requested—Solomon also received. Why? Because his heart was right which resulted in his making the right choice.

This reminds me so much of what Jesus taught us : "But seek first His kingdom, and His righteousness; and all these things shall be added to you" (Matt. 6:33).

When we are willing to seek His kingdom above other things, the Lord provides for our needs. This is exactly what happened to Solomon. He wanted more than anything else to make the right choices at the right time in his life. Without a doubt, he made the right choice when he requested wisdom from the Lord.

Solomon so believed that wisdom was important for living that he recorded, "My son, eat honey, for it is good, yes, the honey from the comb is sweet to your taste; know that wisdom is thus for your soul; if you find it, then there will be a future, and your hope will not be cut off" (Prov. 24:13–14).

He believed just as honey is good for you and sweet to your taste, wisdom is the same for your soul. He believed that if you discover wisdom, your future will be filled with hope and blessing. Yes, Solomon made the right choice.

How Would You Answer That Question?

If the Lord were to allow you to ask Him for anything and told you He would give it to you, for what would you ask? Would your choice indicate spiritual maturity? Would it demonstrate spiritual growth and development? Perhaps our generation would not be as inclined to request wisdom as Solomon was. I have a feeling that many of our generation would ask for money, sex, or power.

Money

Greed is a widespread problem in our country today. It exists as much in the lower and middle classes as it does in the upper class of society. Observing the competitive world of finance and business may sometimes cause you to wonder, "When is enough money enough?" The desire to accumulate possessions consumes the American heart. Materialism has many more followers than the Master, who encouraged us not to seek the treasures on this earth. In fact, Jesus said in Matthew 6:24, "No one can serve two masters; for either he will hate the one and love the other, or he will hold to one and despise the other. You cannot serve God and Mammon."

I believe the Lord was quite clear: our loyalty to Him cannot be shared with money. Money is not wrong until it is the rival for total allegiance to Jesus Christ. If our generation did not ask the Lord for money, it might ask Him for . . .

Sex

Sexual pleasure seems to be the key persuader in American advertising today. Sexual innuendos abound in our society. The power of video images on television and in movies teases our thought life to be filled with a desire for sensual pleasure. Sadly, these messages give a counterfeit understanding of the real meaning of sex.

The end result is that many marital relationships struggle and eventually dissolve, all because of comparison to these vain, self-gratified, manipulated and false images of sex or sexual pleasure. Much of the teenage culture is embracing this view of sex because it is modeled before them by their parents and other heroes in their lives.

If Satan is ineffective in luring us through money or sex, he then tries to create in us a desire for . . .

Power

Pride and ego serve as the drives for power. The mentality of going after what you want, whatever the cost or whoever you have to walk on, is clearly evident in the corporate world of America and its television and movie plots. Power is permissible, even if ethics are compromised.

The kingdom of this world will pass away. All that is accomplished for our ego will pass away. When we invest our lives solely in this world, we are living empty lives. However, we are encouraged through the Word of God to seek the kingdom of God. Above all else, Jesus wants our allegiance to something that will last forever. His kingdom will last for all eternity.

And the Answer Is . . .

If God asked you to request anything you wanted, what would your request be? Would it be money? How about sex or sensual pleasure? Would you request power? All of these choices would result from a coup by Satan in your life—a coup to take you by surprise and deceit.

Let me encourage you to make responsible choices like asking God for wisdom in your life. We cannot afford to make our choices with little thought. We need to ask the Lord for the kind of wisdom that sees life like God sees it, practically making the choices He wants us to make. When this occurs in your life, you will experience the power of a right choice, not the temporary power of this world but the power of God enabling you to live for Him in this world and make a difference for eternity.

I am asked often if it is permissible to pray for yourself. There is nothing wrong with praying for yourself, as long as you pray in accordance with the will of God. One of the ways you can do this is to ask the Lord for wisdom every day of your life. The Bible teaches this in James 1:5: "But if any of you lacks wisdom, let him ask of God, who gives to all men generously and without reproach, and it will be given to him."

God wants to give you His perspective on your life. His perspective will enable you to make the right choices at the right times. This Bible promise in James 1:5 needs to be claimed in our lives for the glory of God. We need to become stakeholders in this verse of hope and promise.

We cannot afford to live our lives as if God does not exist.

Let me suggest that you practice giving God every event of your day. As you consistently follow this suggestion, ask Him for wisdom, for His perspective. Remember, He wants to give this to you; just ask Him.

When we ask the Lord for wisdom, we discover the power of a right choice. Wisdom is always the right choice. We cannot afford spiritually or practically to live our lives as if God does not exist or care. He wants to be involved in every detail of our lives. He is never too busy. You are His interest.

As you daily request wisdom from the Lord, you will discover spiritual power in your life. I believe that as God's wisdom is exercised, His power becomes a compelling force. Therefore, asking Him for wisdom has implications for every area of our lives. His wisdom will not only be better for me, but also for my family, my church, and my job, and will keep the right focus in all areas of my life. I will be a better person when I live life the way God wants me to live it. Spiritual power always follows the right choice.

Requesting wisdom from the Lord daily will also guarantee me a powerful life in eternity. How is this so? When I live my life in His wisdom on this side of heaven, I will be placing my treasures in heaven. My investment will be in eternal things like God, His Word, and people. These will all live forever.

I hope you will join me in making the right choice. Ask for wisdom to see life as God sees it, to make His choice at the right times in your life. Will you choose wisdom above all else in this world? The dividend is awesome—spiritual power.

When we join Solomon and many others by choosing wisdom, we are preparing ourselves to make the proper choices in every area of life, choices which will lead to godliness, real success, and meaningful relationships. What else is there in life? Nothing, really; these are the basics. Let's learn the principles which will grant us these spiritual blessings.

Years ago, when I surrendered my life to preach the gospel of Jesus Christ, I made a wise choice. It was only by the grace of God that at sixteen years of age that choice was the right one. I have doubted many things in life. But one thing I have never doubted is my calling to serve the Lord through preaching.

As I have reflected on that choice, I realize it was a choice made by faith. All our choices are. But the good news is that the God who gives us wisdom is the same God who is the object of our faith. Therefore, we must go step by step with the Lord, one day at a time. This is wisdom being demonstrated spiritually and practically every day of our lives.

We are about to embark on a thrilling journey, a journey that may never leave your life the same, the kind of journey you will share with everyone who sees the evidence in your life of something making an impact in you and through you. Let's journey together and startle the world by making choices which unleash God's power in our lives.

PART TWO

Choices to Godliness

CHOOSING LOVE

CHOOSING REVERENCE

CHOOSING HUMILITY

CHOOSING SELF-CONTROL

CHOOSING PURE MOTIVES

THREE

Choosing Love

It was a foggy morning just a little before 3:00 A.M., over the Big Bayou Canot near Mobile, Alabama, on September 22, 1993. Only three days earlier the railroad bridge over the bayou had undergone its annual inspection. In the midst of the darkness and fog, the MV Mauvilla towboat accidentally pushed one of its barges into the bayou. The errant barge struck and weakened the low bridge. Someone on the tugboat radioed the Coast Guard to inform them of the incident.

Moments later an Amtrak train, the Sunset Limited, reached the bridge. The train was traveling from Los Angeles, California, to Miami, Florida. Unaware of the accident, the Amtrak train crossed over the bridge at seventy miles per hour with 210 passengers on board. The weakened bridge gave way.

As the train derailed, three locomotive units and the first four of the train's eight cars plunged into the alligator-infested bayou. Suddenly, the darkness and fog were thickened by fire and smoke.

The tugboat pilot immediately called in a frantic message to the Coast Guard. The swamp was no longer a quiet place this early morning. Death had invaded its waters.

Many of the passengers survived, but forty-seven did not. Drowning and fire took their lives and sent them into eternity. Not until 5:00 A.M. could help reach the remote disaster area by helicopter. Emergency vehicles were only able to get within six miles of the site on land.

Many heroes emerged that foggy morning. One man, Michael Dopheide, may have saved the lives of thirty passengers. He had just received his tax law degree from DePaul University. This five-foot, ten-inch athlete was heading for Florida after a visit with his sister in California. Jolted out of his sleep, he heard screaming and groaning. As he scrambled through the car hoping to discover an emergency exit, he saw the water rising. He removed the emergency glass and jumped into the swampy waters. He knew he had to help people get out. So he coaxed them one by one to jump six feet down into the water. By treading water in the twenty-five foot deep bayou, he was able to grab their arms when they surfaced. Those who could not swim he towed to a metal girder about ten feet away. The thirty people he helped save included one two-year-old, an elderly lady, and an eleven-year-old girl with cerebral palsy.

Geray and Mary Jane Chancey of Orange Park, Florida, were traveling home with their daughter Andrea, a victim of cerebral palsy. As the water filled their train car, the Chanceys pushed Andrea through a window into the hands of heroic rescuers. This act of love for Andrea was the Chanceys' last act on this earth. They drowned on that September morning in the bayou near Mobile.

The Chanceys' choice brings to mind the remarkable words of Jesus in John 15:13, "Greater love has no one than this, that one lay down his life for his friends."

The Chanceys' choice of love for their daughter may be the greatest human example of love I have ever read or heard about in my life. They loved her with the kind of love Jesus described in this passage. They were willing to give their lives to protect and preserve their daughter's life.

This love was called "greater love," meaning that the greatest act of love anyone could ever demonstrate would be giving his life in exchange for another. It is difficult to comprehend why someone would choose the kind of love that gives his life in the place of another, the kind of love Jesus has for us.

The Meaning of Love

In English there is only one word for love. In Greek and Hebrew, however, there are many. One of these words, *agape*, is used in some form over two hundred times in Scripture. Agape characterizes the essence of who God is. God is love.

Agape love is the highest form of love, the kind of love God has for His Son, Jesus Christ. God also loves us with agape love. What does this mean? It means that God loves us without demanding anything in return. Even though we are unworthy of His love, He chooses to love us.

We are challenged to love God and others in the way God loves us—demanding nothing in return while giving ourselves totally to others.

When God sent Jesus to earth to die for our sins, He did so without requiring anything in return. If no one had responded to Jesus' sacrifice, God still would have sent Jesus to this earth.

Understanding agape love as much as we are able helps us to understand the kind of love God has for us. We are challenged to love God and others in the way God loves us—demanding nothing in return while giving ourselves totally to others.

When the Chanceys saved their daughter's life from the murky waters of that Alabama bayou, they demonstrated agape love. They had nothing to gain and everything, including their lives, to lose. Yet, through *agape* love, they saved Andrea's life and gave their own lives in exchange for hers. This is the highest form of love. This is the way that Jesus loves us.

How Jesus Loves

When we make the choice to love God and others, we are choosing to love God's way. Even though it is difficult to understand the totality of agape love, it is our goal. Choosing love is a step toward being godly, toward becoming more like Christ. To know more about what it means to love God and others, we need an in-depth look at Jesus' love. I believe there are three words which describe how Jesus loves us.

Unconditionally

Jesus loves us unconditionally. What does this mean? It means that He loves us without placing any conditions upon us. Regardless of how we act or conduct ourselves, Jesus loves us. In other words, good conduct does not gain more of God's love.

Jesus was a friend of sinners. One of the first people Jesus brought to Himself was a woman who had been married five times and was, at that time, living with a man outside the bonds of marriage. The last person He brought to Himself was the thief on the cross. Jesus loved both of these people in spite of their personal conduct.

It is so important to understand that we do not earn God's love. Even though my number one goal is to love Him above all else, He loves me as He loves the man who committed adultery last night or the drug addict who slept on one of our city's streets last evening. He does not love me more than He loves you. God's love to all persons is unconditional. When God makes a choice to love me, it is a choice to love me unconditionally.

When we choose to love God, we are to love Him unconditionally. Whether He answers my prayers the way I want Him to or whether He wills what I want Him to will for my life, I am to love God in all circumstances. God is not my puppet; He is the sovereign Lord. My love for Jesus must not depend on what He does in my life or in the world.

Many people struggle with this because they do not see how to love a God who permits suffering or wrong to occur on earth. Much suffering on earth is determined by the wrong choices people make. It is not a reflection of God's character. However, God's character will always show the supremacy of love, agape love, the kind of love given to all persons under all conditions.

If I love the way Jesus loves, I love all persons unconditionally.

A choice to love others is a choice to love them unconditionally. Regardless of how others treat me, I am to love them. Whether someone is good to me or rude to me, each deserves my unconditional love. Expressions of love or of rudeness do not gain or negate my love. If I love the way Jesus loves, I love all persons unconditionally. Choosing this kind of love is a choice to have God's power in my life.

Willfully

Jesus not only loves us unconditionally, but He loves us willfully. This element of agape love means that Jesus loves us because He wants to love us. His desire is to love you and me. Jesus loves us because He wants to love us.

Did God make Jesus go to the cross to die for our sins ? I do not believe He did. I believe Jesus willingly went to the cross so that we might receive forgiveness for our sins and experience eternal life. This kind of love is difficult to comprehend because it is so uncommon, then and today.

The most dreaded disease of Jesus' day was leprosy. When a person contracted leprosy, he became an outcast. His home and clothes were burned. He was exiled to a colony of lepers outside the city. The end result was a slow and painful death. This disease was as feared in Jesus' time as AIDS is feared today.

Most people gave little thought to the lepers, but not Jesus. He loved them unconditionally and willfully. No one made Him pay attention to them. It was not to His advantage physically or politically to give them the time of day. However, Jesus demonstrated agape love to the outcasts of His society. Why? Because He wanted to do so. No one forced Him. He did it out of love.

Our choice to love Jesus is also a willful choice. We do so because we want to love Him. Within our hearts is something that drives us to love Jesus. It is something I want to express to Him, not something I have to do. It is a choice to love Him, a choice made possible by God's power.

We are to love others as we love Jesus—willfully. We are to love people because we want to love them. Whether they are popular or outcasts, we are to love them all. We do this not so they will love us back or help us in some way. Our motives must be pure. I am to love people willfully. This is the way Jesus loves me. I must choose to love others in the same manner.

Sacrificially

Jesus' love for me cost Him everything, including His life. *Agape* love is a sacrificial love, the kind of love that gives me all of God yet exacts nothing in return.

When Jesus was beaten, whipped, and spat upon, His love overflowed with sacrifice. When the crown of thorns was forced onto His brow, His love exhibited sacrifice. When the nails pierced His hands and feet, His love demonstrated sacrifice. His life was poured out for all the world as a sacrifice. Jesus chose to love us sacrificially.

His life was a picture of sacrifice from the time of His birth until the time of His death. When the disciples' immaturity showed so plainly, He loved them sacrificially. When the religious leaders questioned His integrity and His very essence, He never lashed out in anger. When He faced the inequities of His life, He continued giving Himself to God's cause—doing His will and loving us by dying on the cross sacrificially. His choice to love us is a sacrificial choice.

We should be willing to love God sacrificially. Our lives should be poured out as a sacrifice to God everyday. A choice to love Him is a choice to love Jesus sacrificially. This kind of love costs us something. It may cost us our privileges, our desires, our goals, our all. Everything must be placed before Jesus. Our rights are no more; His will must be done. This is the way I choose to love Him sacrificially.

A choice to love God is a choice to love others sacrificially. The "what's in it for me?" philosophy must be ignored.

A choice to love God is a choice to love others sacrificially. A "what's in it for me?" attitude must be ignored. Any relationship of value will involve sacrifice. With time being such a rare commodity, we need to be willing to make time for others. This involves sacrifice. Thoughtfulness involves sacrifice. Sacrifice calls us to move outside ourselves and our comfort zones. It calls us to give our all to others. A choice of love is a choice of sacrifice.

The way Jesus loves us is the way we are to love Him and to love others. As He loves us unconditionally, willfully, and sacrificially, we are to love Him and other people in the same ways. His choice to love us this way is a demonstration of God's power. Our choice to love Him and others in these ways is a choice that will lead us to experience the power of God. This choice toward godliness will enable us to become more like Jesus.

God's Greatest Commandments

The Bible tells of one scribe listening to some people who were trying to challenge Jesus. He recognized that Jesus was answering their questions well. Therefore, he decided to ask Jesus, "What commandment is the foremost of all?" (Mark 12:48). In other words, he wanted to know what God considered the most important commandment to us in this life. Jesus answered this probing question: 'And you shall love the Lord your God with all your heart, and with all your soul, and with all your mind, and with all your strength.' The second is this, 'You shall love your neighbor as yourself.' There is no other commandment greater than these" (Mark 12:30–31).

Jesus answered him in a way he could understand. He did not try to impress him with His oratorical ability. His answer encapsuled the entire Christian life in less than fifty words.

Love God

The challenge of our lives is put to us when we are asked to love God. We are to love Him with every fiber of our being. We are to love Him with all our heart, our soul, our mind, and our strength. Jesus leaves absolutely no part of us out in His answer. He wants us to love God with our all.

Our allegiance is to God above all else. No sporting event or athletic activity is to precede our love for God. No career move should ever precede our love for God. No financial decision should ever jeopardize our love for God. No person should ever take precedence over our love for God.

God wants us to love Him above all others and above all else. In fact, He is grieved whenever He is placed below number one in our lives. He is offended by half-hearted love—the kind of love that just gets by—rather than offering to Him our very best. Our worship, both privately and publicly, should be done with highest excellence. He is God. There is none like Him. Therefore, we must choose not just to love Him, but we must choose to love Him with everything we are and everything we have in life.

Love Others

Jesus did not stop with loving God as the essence of the Christian life. He said we are to love others as we love ourselves.

Therefore, other people are to have the same value to us as we place on ourselves. They are to be treated in the same way that we want others to treat us. As we desire unconditional acceptance, our goal should be unconditional acceptance for every person we meet.

Choosing to love God is not an isolated decision.

This choice to love others is our Christian life being lived out through us and around us. Others will believe we love God only when we love them with the same kind of love that God does. Choosing to love God is not an isolated decision. It will always lead us to loving others in the same way that God loves us.

The Ten Commandments given to Moses on Mount Sinai are summarized in these two great commandments that Jesus gave us. This is the Christian life in its entirety. Our greatest challenges are to love God with everything we are and to love others in the same way we want to be loved. These are God's greatest commandments.

Will You Choose to Love?

We should be willing to practice the teachings of Jesus concerning love. Choosing to love is definitely one of the right choices of life. As you attempt to answer the question, "Will you choose to love?" I want you to consider four very important components of this question.

Will You Choose God?

God is so loving that He has given us the option of whether or not to love Him. He never forces Himself on anyone. He only goes where He is invited.

The main way we choose to love God is to turn from sin and surrender our lives to Jesus Christ as our Lord and Savior. As we make this life-changing choice, we strongly commit to love God. Life is never the same again once Christ comes to live within us.

Another way we choose to love God is to obey His Word. As we read and study His Word, we are challenged to choose to obey it. As we hear it taught or preached, we are again faced with the choice about obedience. Obedience to God's commandments shows Him that we love Him. First John 5:3 says, "For this is the love of God, that we keep His commandments; and His commandments are not burdensome."

Another way we show the Lord we love Him is to be with Him. Time with God is so important. Just as time with your spouse or children indicates your love for them, time spent with God indicates to Him that you love Him. Seek to spend time with Jesus. This is another right choice for your life that will lead you to God's power.

Will You Choose to Love Your Family?

We have a tremendous responsibility to love those that are dearest to us. Our family deserves our utmost commitment of love. Yet, our family may, at times, receive the brunt of our frustrations. They become the sounding boards for our everyday struggles. Do they wonder by our actions whether we really love them? How can we demonstrate love for our families?

The primary way you can show your family love is by demonstrating through word and deed that they are the priority in your life, second only to your personal relationship with Jesus Christ. Your family is more important than your career. They are more important than your job. Your family has priority above personal recreation. They need to know they are your priority.

Spending time with your family is a visible way you choose to demonstrate your love for them. That time may be spent at home together or participating in a recreational activity together. My family loves to attend various activities at a nearby university. We go to basketball and football games together. Whatever brings your family together in a positive environment is evidence of your choice to love them. Nothing can replace time spent as a family. Time builds your family into a team rather than simply a collection of individuals.

Another way to demonstrate love for your family is to share with them that you love them. There are myriad ways to accomplish this goal; however, the best way is to express love verbally to one another. The words "I love you" are music to my ears when my wife and boys share them with me. They motivate me. They encourage me when I am down. Telling your family you love them is a needed practice today.

Showing affection for one another is also so important. I really believe each member of the family needs a hug, a touch, or a kiss every day. I do not believe you ever outgrow the need for signs of affection and words of love for one another. Make the choice to love your family. It is a right and worthy choice.

Will You Choose to Love Your Friends?

I had a man tell me when I was a teenager that if I had five people I could count as real friends, I would be a blessed person. At the time I thought his words were somewhat exaggerated. However, I have learned he was exactly right.

Friends are hard to come by. Friends are people with whom you can be yourself without fearing their judgment or their jeopardizing confidentiality. Friendships go through rough spots just as marriages do. Any friend worth having is worth cultivating and worth the adjustments necessary for that friendship to make it through the course of time.

Two of the greatest friends Jeana and I have ever had are Kirk and Debby Thompson of Springdale, Arkansas. Kirk is president and chief executive officer of J. B. Hunt Transport, which is a $1 billion company. His wife, Debby, stays extremely busy meeting his needs and those of their four children, Nicole, Zachary, Kelsey, and Eden.

Kirk and Debby are approximately the same ages of my wife and me, and Kirk and I have in common a high level of responsibility in our jobs. Jeana and Debby share the priority of the home as the great common denominator of their relationship. Our children have grown up together. We have been close friends since 1986, and we have seen a great deal of transition in their lives in the last several years.

The greatest common bond we share is our love for Jesus Christ and His church. When we are together, honesty prevails. When schedules do not allow us to visit regularly, it seems we just pick up where we left off the last time we were together. Since the first day we met them, Kirk and Debby have permitted Jeana and me to be ourselves. They have loved our children as their own. Money cannot buy what we have shared and learned together over the years.

As adjustments have come into our relationship and transitions have occurred, we have always felt their love and acceptance. They have supported us when our struggles were great, and I believe we supported them in their times of stress as well. We truly have a God-blessed friendship. They truly are the friends who "stick closer than a brother." We love them and they will forever be our friends.

Choose to love your friends. Let them know you love them. Express to them periodically how much you appreciate them. Never take advantage of them or take them for granted. They are blessings from God.

Will You Choose to Love the World's Hurting People?

One of the ministries of our church centers around evangelistic Bible studies conducted in areas of our community such as trailer parks and government-subsidized housing complexes. Our goal is to reach out with the gospel to people who do not come to our worship center. In these Bible studies, we have encountered many hurting and struggling people.

A young man with a drug problem recently accepted Christ as his Savior through the witness of this ministry. His conversion was genuine and he was eager to share his newfound faith and commitment with the church. It was a joyous, heart-warming experience for us all. However, this story doesn't end there. His addiction to drugs did not automatically disappear. His greatest desire was to follow Jesus, yet he lived in an environment that presented constant temptation to return to his old life and habits. He did not have the means to escape it.

Many church folks are rarely exposed to the kind of pain and struggle commonplace in this lifestyle. To comprehend it requires hands-on discipling, remaining in close personal contact, and providing friendship, loving guidance, and encouragement.

I am reminded continually of the hurts and problems people are facing, many of them hard for even me to comprehend. Yet I know that the response Jesus wants me to have to these hurting people is love. Choosing love does have the power to make a difference in the lives of hurting people.

One of the major reasons for so much hurt in our society today is that there are not many parents who love their children like the Chancey couple who gave their lives for their daughter. The parents who daily make the national news are like the couple who left their children at home without parental supervision to take a trip over the holidays or others who have sexually abused their children. Still others neglect their children, allowing them to live in apartments or houses that are dirty and unsanitary. Where are the parents who are doing their jobs the right way? I know many are out there. I wish the national media would feature some of the parents who are choosing to love their children by raising them in the nurture and admonition of the Lord.

Tragically, our world is full of hurting and abused people. What will we do for them? Will we love them? Will we feed them? Will we clothe them? Christian families must take action to raise a generation of children who will truly love the hurting people of our society. Churches have got to leave the comfort of stained glass windows and meet the needs of hurting people.

The challenge before us is not just to love the people of the world we can identify with and easily accept. The challenge is to love the people of this world who no one else is loving. Love must become practical and helpful, meeting the everyday needs of people. This is the essence of the entire gospel of Jesus Christ demonstrated by loving people like Jesus loves them—unconditionally, willfully, sacrificially.

I want to choose love, don't you? Love is God. A gesture of love is a step toward being godly. It is a choice in favor of godliness and opening our lives to God's power. Loving God and loving others is life's meaning and purpose. Nothing more. Nothing less. Just love. Choose love today. Love "believes all things, hopes all things, endures all things. Love never fails" (1 Cor. 13:7–8).

F O U R

Choosing Reverence

Disappointment had invaded their marriage on several occasions. More than anything, they wanted a child. Their attempts were in vain and their dreams seemed to die.

Confusion filled the husband's heart. He could not understand why the Lord would not give them the blessing of a child. His bewilderment deepened when he thought back to the words God shared with him before he left his homeland. Genesis 12:2–3 records that message, "And I will make you a great nation, and I will bless you, and make your name great; and so you shall be a blessing; and I will bless those who bless you, and the one who curses you I will curse. And in you all the families of the earth shall be blessed."

Abraham and his wife Sarah must have thought back on those words on numerous evenings together. They probably asked one another and the Lord, "How will all of the families of the earth be blessed if we cannot have children?"

After years of frustration from not being able to conceive and see the Lord's promise come true, Sarah decided to give her maid, Hagar, to Abraham. She reasoned that if Hagar could give Abraham children, God could fulfill His promise. So, at eighty-six years of age, Abraham became a father to the son of Hagar. They named him Ishmael.

This did not solve Sarah's problem. She came to despise Hagar and treated her so harshly that Hagar left Sarah's presence. However, the angel of the Lord appeared to Hagar and told her to return and submit to Sarah. Sarah had to live with her choice to get ahead of God by giving Hagar to Abraham.

At age ninety-nine, Abraham heard from the Lord again, and again the Lord reaffirmed His covenant with Abraham. The Lord told him he would still be the father of many nations. Abraham received these words with faith even though he did not understand how God was going to fulfill His word to him.

When the word finally came that ninety-year-old Sarah would have a child, she laughed to herself. In the midst of her laughter the Lord asked, "Is there anything too difficult for the Lord?" (see Gen. 18:14). Stunned by the question, Sarah denied she had laughed. She knew God had to plan something miraculous and did not want to miss it.

Just as the Lord had told them, the promise became a reality. At age ninety, Sarah had a baby, and Abraham, one hundred years old, became a father. Once again the Lord brought real joy to Sarah's life. The hurt, pain, and disappointment were gone. She was a mother. Her dream and God's promise had come true.

Abraham was thrilled to know that through Isaac all of his descendants would be named. He must have remembered the times when the Lord had shared those promises with him. He probably was ashamed that he became impatient with the Lord and had a child with Hagar. What was done was done. It was time now to see how God's promise was to be fulfilled.

Abraham was filled with deep love and gratitude toward God, especially now that God had fulfilled His promise. However, was his love deep enough to do what God was calling him to do? The challenges had been many in his life, but now it seemed in his advanced years the greatest challenge was before him. The Bible records in Genesis 22:1–2 what the Lord asked of him:

> Now it came about after these things, that God tested Abraham, and said to him, "Abraham!" And he said, "Here I am." And He said, "Take now your son, your only son, whom you love, Isaac, and go to the land of Moriah; and offer him there as a burnt offering on one of the mountains of which I will tell you."

What a request! The Lord was asking Abraham to offer his son on the altar. Without hesitation, Abraham chose to obey God and began his three-day journey to Moriah. It must have been a very long journey. What would Sarah say if he returned without Isaac? What would Isaac say when he understood he was to be the sacrifice? Abraham could not turn back. He knew he must obey God and yet must have wondered how God would fulfill his promise if Isaac was dead. He knew that if the Lord wanted him to kill Isaac He could also raise him from the dead. His faith was great. He kept relying on the promise.

What motivated Abraham to walk up that mountain to offer Isaac as a sacrifice? He reverenced his Lord, and stood in awe of His greatnes. Abraham told those accompanying him that he and Isaac would go the rest of the way by themselves. He declared these words of faith, "We will worship and return to you" (Gen. 22:5). Together, he and Isaac walked toward the place of sacrifice. Carrying the wood, Isaac asked his father, "Where is the sacrifice?" Abraham responded to him and said, "God will provide."

Abraham built the altar, bound Isaac to it and took the knife into his hand to slay his only son. But suddenly, Abraham heard his name called. The Lord spoke to him through an angel, "Do not stretch out your hand against the lad, and do nothing to him;

for now I know that you fear God, since you have not withheld your son, your only son, from me" (Gen. 22:12).

Because Abraham chose to reverence God, the Lord did not require him to offer his son. Instead, He provided a ram in a thicket. Abraham named the place, "The Lord Will Provide" (see v. 14). The Lord reaffirmed His promise that through Isaac all of the nations would be blessed.

Abraham chose to revere the Lord his God. His choice was not easy. To place Isaac on the altar was a direct indication that he loved God more than he loved Isaac. This is what the Lord wants from each of us. He wants us to choose daily to revere Him, to stand in awe of Him. This story of worship is one of the greatest in all of the Scriptures. Why is this so?

One of the highest forms of worship is making right choices. Abraham's worship was accepted because he made the right choice. He did not attempt to negotiate with God or to compromise. His placing Isaac on the altar demonstrated his love for God. Imagine the reverence Abraham must have had for his God, so much that he was willing to sacrifice his son. This choice was a high and acceptable form of worship.

When God Is Not Reverenced

Have you ever considered what happens when we do not choose to reverence God in our lives? The opposite of what we have learned about Abraham is described in Romans 3:10–18:

> There is none righteous, not even one; there is none who understands, there is none who seeks for God; all have turned aside, together they have become useless; there is none who does good, there is not even one. Their throat is an open grave, with their tongues they keep deceiving, the poison of asps is under their lips; whose mouth is full of cursing and bitterness; their feet are swift to shed blood, destruction and

misery are in their paths, and the path of peace have they not known. There is no fear of God before their eyes.

Did you notice that last sentence? The reason the list of sins is so great and so long is because the people did not fear or revere the Lord.

For the sake of emphasis and clarity, permit me to paraphrase what the writer is saying:

There is no fear of God before their eyes. There is none righteous, not even one; there is no fear of God before their eyes. There is none who understands; there is none who seeks for God because there is no fear of God before their eyes. All have turned aside. Together they have become useless. There is none who does good, not even one because there is no fear of God before their eyes. Their throat is an open grave; with their tongues they keep deceiving, and the poison of asps is under their lips because there is no fear of God before their eyes. Their mouths are full of cursing and bitterness because there is no fear of God before their eyes. Their feet are swift to shed blood because there is no fear of God before their eyes. Destruction and misery are in their paths because there is no fear of God before their eyes. And the path of peace have they not known because there is no fear of God before their eyes.

If people do not fear or revere God, they have the potential to commit any kind of sin.

Did you get the point? If people do not fear God, they have the potential to commit any kind of sin. Choosing to reverence God will spare us a lifestyle that does not honor God and will eventually destroy us. Since reverence is a high form of worship, failure to reverence God is an act of worshiping ourselves.

Great blessing is given to those who choose to reverence God; therefore, we need to understand what this means.

What Is Reverence?

In corporate worship, we sometimes equate being reverent with being quiet and reserved in our expression during worship. At times reverence in public worship may be exhibited in this way; however, this is not the real meaning of the word.

Reverence is standing in awe of who God is. Reverence is my response to the majesty of God. Reverence is my recognition that God is all-powerful. There is none like Him.

Being still before the Lord, meditating on who He is and what He can do, is a high form of worship.

When Moses was in the remote parts of the desert, he noticed a burning bush and was intrigued when the bush was not consumed by the fire. As he drew near, he heard his name called, "Moses, Moses!" Moses responded and said, "Here I am." In Exodus 3:5–6, we read what took place next: "Then He said, 'Do not come near here; remove your sandals from your feet, for the place on which you are standing is holy ground.' He said also, 'I am the God of your father, the God of Abraham, the God of Isaac, and the God of Jacob.' Then Moses hid his face, for he was afraid to look at God."

Moses was in the presence of God. He could not look into the glory of the Lord's face. His fear was godly fear—a reverence for God. He removed his sandals. He hid his face. He experienced the majesty of God in a personal way. From this spiritual posture of reverence, God called him to lead the people of Israel out of their slavery in Egypt.

When we choose to reverence God, it is a high form of worship whether experienced privately or publicly. Being still before the Lord, meditating on who He is and what He can do, is a high form of worship. To stand in awe of God for who He is and what He is able to do is a great choice to make in life.

When worship in a local church concentrates on the majesty of God and the power of God, then reverencing God will take place in public worship. From this spiritual posture of reverence, God will call us into the world to make a difference for Him, just like He did Moses. When we reverence God, it is an immediate response to His awesome person and presence. There is no other reasonable response when you are before the living God except to reverence Him. So choose to reverence God.

The Benefits of Reverencing God

The spiritual blessings of God always follow the right choices that we make in life. Choosing to reverence God is no different. The benefits of reverencing Him are numerous.

Choosing Reverence Is the Beginning of Wisdom

Wisdom is choosing to see life as God sees it and responding to life in the way He wants you to respond. Wisdom from the Lord is a result of choosing to reverence God. When I am willing to stand in awe of who He is and what He can do, I will gain His wisdom. The Bible says in Proverbs 1:7, "The fear of the Lord is the beginning of knowledge; fools despise wisdom and instruction."

Any truth we learn about how life should be lived will be acquired from the Lord. Any knowledge worth knowing is preceded by a godly fear of the Lord.

Since real wisdom and knowledge are available only from the Lord, people who refuse to stand in awe of Him are regarded by God as fools. The world may give them great adulation or fame as they acquire a path of luxury, success, great wealth, but God sees their headstrong actions and selfishness leading them down the path of destruction. Their intractable spirit scorns the idea of seeing life the way God sees it and making the choices He would want them to make in life.

There are many people in our country today who laugh at the thought of living their lives according to the principles of

Scripture and ridicule those who choose to live by these principles. Think about it for a moment. What is their problem? Is it their philosophy of life? Is it their worldview? Their problem is that they do not reverence the Lord.

While the fools of this world ignore who God is and what He says to them about life, the wise are eager to obey His instruction. "Give instruction to a wise man, and he will be still wiser, teach a righteous man, and he will increase his learning. The fear of the Lord is the beginning of wisdom, and the knowledge of the Holy One is understanding" (Prov. 9:9–10).

> *When we choose to reverence God in our lives, we are going to see life the way God sees it and make the right choices.*

When we choose to reverence God in our lives, we are going to see life the way God sees it and make the right choices. The first and foremost step into wisdom and understanding is to fear the Lord. When we learn about God and who He is, we are moving toward understanding more about life.

A wise person will always receive instruction. A wise person realizes that wisdom is a process, that one can become wiser. Do not forget that the experience of receiving wisdom begins with reverencing the Lord.

When you face the dilemma of decision making, where does the process begin? It should begin in the presence of the Lord, reverencing Him. It is the first step toward our priority of discerning His will for our lives. Choosing reverence is the beginning of wisdom.

Choosing Reverence Brings Strong Confidence

In today's world we are told that mind-power, self-esteem, and a positive attitude are the keys to facing all that life brings us. People around the world are buying these lies. They are joining groups that encourage them in these vain pursuits. They are paying major dollars to learn these concepts in seminar settings. Even certain churches are counterfeiting the message of the gospel by propagating these deceitful attempts of man to master life successfully.

I am well aware of the power of the human mind, the value of self-esteem, and what a positive attitude can do for a person. My problem with using these artificial criteria as the keys to a successful life is that they cannot stand alone. When people face traumatic experiences, they are in a hopeless situation if all they have is mind-power, self-esteem, and a positive attitude.

What gives us strong confidence in life? We need to live in godly fear of the Lord. The Bible says, "In the fear of the Lord there is strong confidence, and His children will have refuge. The fear of the Lord is a fountain of life, that one may avoid the snares of death" (Prov. 14:26–27). The only way to face the adversities of life is to have strong confidence in the Lord. This confidence comes from the belief that God is sovereign and in control of absolutely everything.

A choice to reverence God is a choice to show strong confidence in Him. Regardless of the winds of adversity that may blow our way, reverencing the Lord will give us confidence that God is in control. As the source of our lives, He nourishes us when we walk through trouble, even trouble as extreme as the shadow of death. Our safety in the midst of trouble is found solely in our God. It is not found in mind-power, self-esteem, or a positive attitude.

The only way to face the adversities of life is to have strong confidence in the Lord.

If confidence is lacking in your life, perhaps you need to place yourself in the powerful presence of God. As we stand in awe of who He is and what He is able to do, we are able to walk through life with confidence. It is obvious that the apostle Paul understood this principle when he penned these words found in Philippians 4:13, "I can do all things through Him who strengthens me."

This "can do" spirit existed because of the strong confidence Paul had gained through reverencing the Lord. We see it demonstrated through his life he recorded in Romans 8:37–39.

> But in all these things we overwhelmingly conquer through Him who loved us. For I am convinced that neither death, nor life, nor angels, nor principalities, nor things present, nor things to come, nor powers, nor height, nor depth, nor any other created thing, shall be able to separate us from the love of God, which is in Christ Jesus our Lord.

A conquering spirit occurs when there is confidence in the Lord. Reverencing God brings strong confidence in your life.

Reverencing God Results in a Prolonged, Exciting Life

People today are more committed to physical fitness and proper diet than ever before. Why is this so? There is a craze in America today to live a long, full life. Through advancements in medical technology, people are achieving this goal as lifespans increase. We know that proper diet and a regular exercise program can lengthen our lives.

While these factors can contribute to giving us more time on this earth and a better quality of life, they carry no guarantee for us. The Lord still determines our length of days and the quality of our lives.

Does reverencing the Lord have anything to do with the length of your days on this earth? Yes! The Bible says in Proverbs 10:27, "The fear of the Lord prolongs life, but the years of the wicked will be shortened." In this verse, the Lord contrasts a godly life with a wicked life, teaching us that reverencing Him extends our earthly life. Conversely, a wicked lifestyle shortens life because of the power of sin and its destructive toll on the human body.

The chorus goes, "Anybody here want to live forever, say I do." This chorus could be changed and be sung, "Anybody here want to live longer, just reverence the Lord."

Excitement in life is a goal most people desire. This excitement is dependent on your relationship to God. If you do not know the Lord in a personal way, then you may think that excitement is found only in the options the world has to offer. If you have a personal relationship with God through Jesus Christ, then you are aware that an exciting life results from living in obedience to God and His Word.

We discover this principle in Proverbs 4:20–23, "My son, give attention to my words; incline your ear to my sayings. Do not let them depart from your sight; keep them in the midst of your heart. For they are life to those who find them, and health to all their whole body. Watch over your heart with all diligence, for from it flow the springs of life."

When we take to heart the words of the Lord, we experience life. In fact, health extends throughout our bodies.

Without a doubt, I live an exciting life when, like Mary of Bethany long ago, I sit at His feet in reverence, listen to His words, and obey Him. "The fear of the Lord leads to life, so that one may sleep satisfied, untouched by evil" (Prov. 19:23). Our lives are filled with excitement, peace, and safety when we choose to reverence the Lord.

We should take care of our bodies and do all we can to have good health. However, let others place their hope for a long and exciting life in bodily exercise and diet alone. We are different! As His children, we are able to be in His presence daily, reverencing Him. One of the many benefits for us will be to experience a prolonged and exciting life.

Reverencing God Provides a Promising Future

People are consumed with a desire to know their future. They attempt to chart their lives in a way that will provide them a promising future, often relying on forecasters whose predictions touch all areas of life and business.

I believe my future is determined by the Lord. When I make the choice to reverence Him, He promises a rewarding future. It is not my role to chart my course through the murky waters of life, it is His, for He sees the dangerous places I cannot see.

Therefore, my trust must be only in the Lord, not in some futurist or forecaster. The trends of the world are not necessarily the trends of my future. The Bible says, "Do not let your heart envy sinners, but live in the fear of the Lord always. Surely there is a future, and your hope will not be cut off " (Prov. 23:17–18).

My life does not operate by the same principles as those who do not know God. My challenge is to live in reverence of the Lord, to be in His presence, observing who He is. This spiritual discipline promises me a future filled with hope.

This promising future may not be what I thought it would be, but it will be what God grants me. Therefore, my future is filled with promise and hope. Hopelessness does not exist in the person who reverences the Lord. Reverencing God provides a promising future for you and me.

How You Can Reverence the Lord

Understanding what it means to reverence the Lord benefits the followers of Jesus in extraordinary ways. I hope these simple, practical suggestions will help you understand how you can reverence the Lord. These daily choices you can make will place you in the wonderful and astounding presence of the Lord and will help you consistently choose to reverence God in your life.

Lean on God Daily

Let God be the support of your life. We lean on the Lord when we place a priority on spending time with Him every day. This is the most important appointment to keep daily.

Do you spend time alone with God every day? Is it consistent? Is it meaningful? In my book, *Reconnecting,* the entire first section is committed to challenging Christians to spend daily time with God. Several practical suggestions are provided there to help a person gain consistency in a daily time with God.

Please do not disregard this principle as shallow or for beginners only. I am talking about the key to your spiritual survival. There is no way you will ever live for Christ without spending time with God. Choosing godliness in your life will occur only if you are leaning on God daily through a personal quiet time with Him and letting Him have a chance to make a positive difference in your life.

When trials come your way and the winds of adversity seem to be blowing at hurricane force, the only sustaining power you have is the Lord. However, His power will only be experienced in your life to the degree you are committed to be with Him in daily moments of privacy. He longs to have you in His presence. Leaning on God daily is one simple suggestion how to reverence the Lord in your life.

Live a Holy Life

In your journey toward godliness, you will learn that our God is a holy God. He is not in need of us, but we are in need of Him. Yes, He is a holy God.

Numerous Scriptures encourage us to live a life of holiness. One of them is 1 Peter 1:14–16, "As obedient children, do not be conformed to the former lusts which were yours in your ignorance, but like the Holy One who called you, be holy yourselves also in all your behavior; because it is written, 'You shall be holy, for I am holy.'"

Now that we have been changed by the power of Christ, we are not to be linked to our former sins committed when we were unbelievers. Now that we have responded to the Lord's call to salvation, we are to become like Him—holy! Our behavior and our choices in life should represent the One who called us. To be like Jesus is to be holy.

It takes time to be holy. It is a process of continual transformation of our lives. We do not wake up one day and realize that we are holy! This process of being changed into the likeness of Jesus Christ is determined by our choices. Choose to reverence the Lord in your life by living a holy life, a life like Jesus Christ's.

Love the Experience of Worship on the Lord's Day

The experience of public worship in a local church is so strategic in the Christian's life. Whether we sing the great hymns of the faith that echo the majesty of God or the contemporary choruses of our day that make us aware of His eternal presence, or hear Bible preaching that ushers us literally into the presence of God, we have been helped to reverence our Lord.

There may be times when you need to be alone with God, but on the Lord's Day, Scripture encourages us to be in our local church worshiping the exalted and coming Christ. The dynamic of being with God's people in a powerful worship experience should never be underestimated or minimized. The experience of hearing God's Word explained and applied to our lives will only push us toward our goal of showing reverence to God.

Do not be swayed or deceived by the prevalent convictions of many that the church is insignificant. Discover a church making a difference in your area, a church that will encourage you to make the right choice to reverence God in your life. One of the ways you can reverence the Lord is to love the experience of worship on the Lord's Day in your local church.

Making right choices in life is a form of worship. Choosing to reverence God in your life is worship in its highest form.

Make the right choice today. Spend time with God. Stand in awe of who He is and what He is able to do. This choice of reverence will place you in the company of persons like Abraham, Moses, and Paul. But more than that, it will place you in the presence of Almighty God. You will never be the same again.

FIVE

Choosing Humility

Humility is one of the most difficult subjects to write about or discuss with others. If someone says he is humble, then questions are raised about his spiritual authenticity. If someone says he is not humble, then he admits his sinfulness. After prayer and thought, I have decided to share with you openly the struggles I have with humility.

I know a great deal more about the opposite of humility—pride. My sinful nature is bent toward pride much more than it is toward humility. You have heard about the guy who shared a few testimonial words in the Sunday evening service, saying, "I want everyone here tonight to know I am proud that I am a humble man." I believe I may know that man!

I struggle with humility because it will not permit me to promote myself. There is something within my nature that really enjoys exalting myself. Do you ever have that problem? It is difficult to suppress my desire to tell others my accomplishments, particularly when they parade their accomplishments before me. Sometimes I want to stand up and say, "Look what I did!" I do not want to be that way, but my pride seems to be more dominant than my humility.

Humility does not have to prove itself to others. Yet at times I want others to know I am a pretty spiritual guy. I tend to excuse this as a pastoral tendency because I think people expect me to be that way; however, my human nature wants to make sure others know of spiritual acts I have done or experiences I have had. We are to speak about the work of Christ in our lives. The heart of the issue lies in our motives. I have to ask myself, "Why do I want others to know what God is doing in my life or what I have experienced spiritually recently?" Pride would excuse a false motive and stand to give itself attention. Sometimes I wonder if anyone struggles with this as I do.

It does not matter to a humble person whether anyone knows who they are or not. My pride prompts me to insure that others know who I am. I want to be somebody, whatever that means. The old nature wants people to know who I am and what I have done in my life. In my heart, my desire is only to be what God wants me to be in life.

Humility does not have to have the last word, but pride always has to have the last word on any issue. This is a real struggle for me. It seems to come out at home with my family more than anywhere else, but my nature is to always make sure I have the last word. It is as though I cannot be content until I say that final word on the subject, especially if the issue is a hot one! This is where my pride exalts itself the most. I am praying for God to tame my tongue, but oh, what a miracle it will take in my life for this to happen.

Humility is seen in a person's spirit, but pride is revealed through attitudes like arrogance, haughtiness, and conceit. I have known this is a problem in my life a long time, and have experienced some victory over it, but the struggle is still there.

Humility always places value on other people, but pride excels in putting others down. I really value other people. I work hard at accepting others the way they are. Yet, at times, my pride fills me with so much bad information that I fail at this point. Then I follow suit with others who think more highly of themselves than they ought to think. The result is that others get put down and devalued.

Of all the struggles I have with my pride, this aspect makes me want to conquer my shortcoming more than any other. I know in my heart that I am the least of all persons. I am better than no one else. It irritates me so much when others are put down because of my pride.

Well, many of you may want to put down this book now and never pick it up again. You may be thinking, "If I knew this guy was like this, I would never have purchased this book." I will be the first to admit to you—I am just a man. Proud. Carnal. Sinful. If that disappoints you, then you need to stick to the only book that is God-breathed—the Bible. It is a perfect book written by a perfect God.

Certainly, I do not need to remind you that all who served God by writing the Scriptures under the inspiration of the Spirit were sinful people. They were simply vessels of God. His inspiration and breath separated the truth from their human error. Do not misunderstand me. I have the highest regard for each of them. However, the Bible is God's Book. It was breathed into existence by Him.

The human personalities that God used to put the Bible together were just like ours. They struggled with pride. I can really identify with them. Oh, not in the way God breathed His Words through them—that was totally unique. But out of my openness with you about my struggles, maybe God will speak to you about pride in your life, too.

I meet people every day, and I know people are not different than I. Pride may be our biggest problem. It has the power to choke the life of God out of us. I am confident that you can identify with my struggles with pride.

My personal desire is to be filled with humility, not pride. I want to be like Jesus, the only example of humility that I know. Even though this is my desire, pride gets in my way. Can it be shattered? Can my pride be placed under control? Yes! I hesitate to say there are times I am living in humility, but I can tell you there are times when my pride is under the control of the Holy Spirit. Therefore, to suppress pride is to live in humility. God is our only hope for this to take place.

I have met many wonderful people in my life. Yet, I would be hesitant to describe any of them as the picture of humility. Even the apostle Paul only gave Jesus Christ as the example of a humble servant. Therefore, I place before you the only person I know who always demonstrates a spirit of humility and never is consumed with a passion of pride. His name —Jesus Christ.

A Picture of Humility

Humility is almost a missing word in our language and lifestyle today. Our society is consumed with a "what's in it for me" philosophy. In other words, many people in the world are not interested in anything unless it will help them in some way. The spirit of taking is more a part of our society than giving. Therefore, to talk about humility runs against the total philosophy of this world. It is a foreign subject to most people, except Jesus Christ.

Humility was a way of life for Jesus. He began His life in a lowly manner by being born in a stable. He lived His life in humility as He identified with all persons, never placing one above another. He died in humility. He was brought low by the scorn of His society. Finally, He was executed on a cross, the most humiliating way to die in His day. Jesus lived a life of love, service, and sacrifice. He is the perfect picture of humility.

One of the events in Jesus' life that is so filled with moving emotion is an event that pictures humility. It occurred during Passion Week, the last week of His earthly life. His hour of real suffering was about to begin. His mind must have been focused on the cross, but still His heart was focused on His followers.

The disciples were special friends to our Lord. Each of them had left their jobs and families to assist Him in the work of the kingdom of God. Jesus "loved them to the end" (John 13:1). Even though Judas Iscariot had already opened his heart to Satan's prodding to betray the Lord, Jesus still loved Judas. In these final hours the Lord wanted to demonstrate to His followers one more time what He had tried to teach them in their three-year journey with Him. It was a review of His entire life with them. The Bible records this event in John 13:3–5,

> Jesus, knowing that the Father had given all things into His hands, and that He had come forth from God, and was going back to God, rose from supper, and laid aside His garments; and taking a towel, girded Himself about. Then He poured water into the basin, and began to wash the disciples' feet, and to wipe them with the towel with which He was girded.

It was the practice in Jesus' day that a servant would wash the feet of a dinner guest before eating. However, this night Jesus was the servant who washed the feet of His followers. Peter was astounded that the Lord was going to wash his feet. In fact, Peter said to Him, "Never shall you wash my feet!" (John 13:8). The Lord responded with a direct reply, "If I do not wash you, you have no part with Me" (v. 8).

How this statement must have stunned Peter. No part of the Lord? No! Therefore we read in verse 9, "Simon Peter said to Him, 'Lord, not my feet only, but also my hands and my head.'" Peter did not want just a part of Jesus. He wanted all of Jesus. Of all the disciples, Peter probably struggled with pride as much as any of them. Yet, his heart desired humility. He wanted to be like Jesus in every way. This is why he declared to the Lord that he wanted Him to wash his hands and his head.

Humility is no respecter of persons. Can you imagine Jesus kneeling down at the feet of Judas Iscariot? He knew that Satan had already turned Judas's heart against Him. Still, our Lord washed the feet of the one who would betray Him. What a picture of love and humility to follow.

> *To be like Jesus is to be a humble servant, willing to meet needs by serving others. Could this be our highest service to God?*

Why did Jesus decide to wash the disciples' feet? I believe the answer to this question is found in John 13:13–15, when Jesus said, "You call Me Teacher and Lord; and you are right; for so I am. If I then, the Lord and the Teacher, washed your feet, you also ought to wash one another's feet. For I gave you an example that you should do as I did to you." He was modeling a lifestyle of humility and service and teaching them that since they were no greater than He, they should serve each other even as He had served them.

To be like Jesus is to be a humble servant, willing to meet needs by serving others. Could this be our highest service to God? If the greatest thing the Teacher did for His followers was to serve them with humility, then how can I decline to pursue a life of service to others? Could the depth of our spirituality be seen through our level of service to other people? Absolutely! Humility fixes our eyes on others, not ourselves. Jesus is the perfect picture of humility.

Humility is not an easy choice. The price is high and sometimes painful. However, to choose humility is to choose to be like Jesus. It is a high choice to serve others and to place them above yourself. It is a choice to lower yourself in every way. It is a choice to give yourself away, not expecting anything in return.

Again, it is a choice to be like Jesus. When we choose not to be like Jesus we choose a life of pride rather than humility. Since I have shared with you a picture of humility through the life of Jesus, perhaps we need to see what happens in the lives of those who choose pride.

Pride is not just a willful, selfish choice. It is dangerous, like playing with fire. Pride will burn you, according to the Scriptures. Therefore, let's be aware of this subtle and destructive enemy within us. Let's consider what happens when we choose pride rather than humility. Perhaps this may motivate us to choose Jesus' way of humility rather than our way of pride.

The Progression of Pride

Where does pride take you ultimately? The Bible speaks to the destination of pride in Proverbs 16:18, saying, "Pride goes before destruction, and a haughty spirit before stumbling." The ultimate destination of pride is destruction. This destruction will occur in the person's life who is filled with pride.

Just as Jesus comes to my mind when thinking about humility, King Saul comes to mind when thinking about pride. Saul wasted much of his life because of his unrestrained pride. He never seemed to be able to put a bridle on his personal desires. He never made this needed choice in his life. It cost him so much, including the kingship and eventually, his life.

Selfishness

Personal pride always results in selfishness. Saul was no exception to this rule. One time, due to his pride, he demonstrated bad judgment by brashly offering the burnt offering Samuel was appointed to make. Out of selfishness and an exalted ego, Saul decided he should make the offering. In 1 Samuel 13:13–14, we read what Samuel told Saul because he made the offering:

And Samuel said to Saul, "You have acted foolishly; you have not kept the commandment of the Lord your God, which He commanded you, for now the Lord would have established your kingdom over Israel forever. But now your kingdom shall not endure. The Lord has sought out for Himself a man after his own heart, and the Lord has appointed him as ruler over His people, because you have not kept what the Lord commanded you."

Saul's selfish action cost him the kingdom.

When we choose selfishness, it is a costly choice. We end up bringing attention to ourselves rather than to God. While humility points people to God, selfishness points people to us.

Disobedience to God

The Lord told Saul to kill Amalek and destroy all he had. When Saul engaged in this battle, he was successful; however, he spared Agag, the king of Amalek, and brought back the best the people of Amalek had. Saul was obedient to an extent, but not fully obedient to God.

The Lord responded to Saul's action through his spokesman Samuel. "And Samuel said, 'Has the Lord as much delight in burnt offerings and sacrifices as in obeying the voice of the Lord? Behold, to obey is better than sacrifice, and to heed than the fat of rams'" (1 Sam. 15:22). God was not pleased with Saul because he had not followed all God told him to do. The Lord did not want him to sacrifice, but to obey Him fully.

Partial Obedience

There is such an important spiritual principle in this story. We need to remember: Partial obedience is the most subtle form of disobedience. Anytime we do not fully obey God in our lives, we are being disobedient to Him. Saul's choice to disobey God was a choice emerging out of the pride in his life. He thought he had a better idea than God.

God determines what we do in life. I am here to carry out His plan fully, whatever that plan may be. God does not accept my choice to be partially obedient to Him. My choice to partially obey equals outright disobedience to God.

Rebellion Against Authority

As we continue to think about the progression of pride, be aware of its deceitfulness. The Lord was not pleased with the choices Saul made. First Samuel 15:23 reads, "For rebellion is as the sin of divination, and insubordination is as iniquity and idolatry. Because you have rejected the word of the Lord, He has also rejected you from being king." The progression of pride in Saul's life went from selfishness to disobedience to God and here to rebellion against authority.

Anytime we choose disobedience to God, we are in rebellion against God.

Saul's disrespect for God's authority was compared to iniquity and idolatry. Saul's pride led him to idolize his own desires rather than God's. He was rejecting the Lord's instructions for his life; therefore, God rejected him as king.

Anytime we choose disobedience to God, we are in rebellion against God. A choice for myself is usually a choice against God. God's will has to be superior to my will at all times in my life. If it is not, then my pride will deceive me to rebel against God's authority in my life.

A Life Without Spiritual Power

Saul's rebellion opened his life to the attack of Satan. The Bible says, "Now the Spirit of the Lord departed from Saul, and an evil spirit from the Lord terrorized him" (1 Sam. 16:14). Saul lost his spiritual power all because of his choice to exalt himself.

Each of us has a choice. Will we live our lives in God's power or will we live in our own power? Whenever we choose pride over humility, then we are choosing to live in our own power. The result is that our enemy, Satan, will attack us and bring his forces against us. Our pride will result, at this point, in a lack of spiritual power.

Jealousy and Anger

David was chosen as Saul's successor. This young warrior had returned from battling the Philistine, Goliath, and people were heralding his unbelievable victory. They were singing, "Saul has slain his thousands, and David his ten thousands" (1 Sam. 18:7). Jealousy and anger filled the heart of Saul. From that day on, he did not trust David. There were occasions when even attempted to kill David.

Only a choice to save your own face will make you be filled with jealousy and anger toward another person. This immature choice of pride will cause multiple heartaches in life. There will always be others who will have things that you will never have. There will always be others who will receive more praise than you receive. Being jealous of them and eventually acting in anger toward them is not the correct choice. The correct choice is to be like Jesus. Humility chooses to honor others. Pride only desires to honor self.

An Association with the Demonic

I wish the progression of pride would stop, but it does not. Pride never gets enough. Pride caused Saul to panic before his battle with the Philistines. He needed some help so he went to a fortuneteller, a story told in 1 Samuel 28. How unfortunate that he would stoop to receiving assistance from a fortune-teller, an agent of the demonic instead of God. Surely the Lord was sorry for the day He permitted Saul to be king.

An obsession with self results in an obsession to know your future. There is a trend in our society today to be intrigued with the powers of darkness. Many place great emphasis on astrology and the power the stars have in determining their future. It is the same selfish curiosity which plunged Saul into associating with the demonic forces.

Let God determine your future. Do not let your choice of pride ruin your life and influence. Choose humility. It can only be discovered at one place. That place is at the feet of Jesus.

Suicide

The taking of one's own life is a very self-centered act. Some cannot face what they believe to be insurmountable obstacles. They see their problems as the greatest anyone has ever known. They see their struggles as the most difficult anyone has ever had. As a result they take their own life rather than face their own humanity.

Read about Saul taking his own life after he was wounded. "Then Saul said to his armor bearer, 'Draw your sword and pierce me through with it, lest these uncircumcised come and pierce me through and make sport of me.' But his armor bearer would not, for he was greatly afraid. So Saul took his sword and fell on it" (1 Sam. 31:4).

Even as he faced death, Saul, full of pride, preferred to take his own life rather than face humiliation and death at the hand of his enemies. Life is never bad enough to end it on your own. Those who do leave a legacy of pain and hurt for all who love them dearly. Do not let your pride keep you from getting the help you need. Let your friends, your family members, or some professional know of your pain.

Always ignore and reject a choice made from pride. It always progresses into something far beyond what you ever imagined. Greater persons than you have fallen as its prey.

Saul's life warns us of the dangers of pride. Even though a willingness to be second and a willingness to serve others does not come easily for any of us, choosing humility is far better than choosing pride. Pride leads toward destruction, but where does humility lead us?

The Power of Humility

Jesus' life overflowed with humility. His humility gave Him great power in relating to others.

When we choose humility, we experience a certain power in our lives. It occurs because humility is always a step toward living like Jesus. What fruit does this power bear in our lives?

Honor

A spirit of humility always brings honor to the Lord and will eventually bring honor to your life. While pride brings destruction, humility brings honor. The Bible says in Proverbs 29:23, "A man's pride will bring him low, but a humble spirit will obtain honor."

> *A spirit of humility always brings honor to the Lord and will eventually bring honor to your life.*

An interesting paradox is posed in this Scripture. While the world would tell us to never be shy about our greatness and accomplishments, God says to be humble in spirit and, in time, He will bring honor to our lives.

In our vain attempts to receive the world's applause, we desire the honor of others. We want them to treat us as though we have value—like we are someone special! The Bible affirms in Proverbs 15:33 that "before honor comes humility."

As a college student seeking direction from God about my life and ministry, I was drawn to Psalm 75:6–7: "For not from the east, nor from the west, nor from the desert comes exaltation, but God is the Judge; He puts down one, and exalts another."

These verses have served as my life verses. I do not wish to play the games of men in promoting myself or the ministry to which God has called me. If He wants to do something new with me, He knows I desire to know it and to do it. Only He determines who is exalted and who is not. Yet God is faithful to honor the person who comes before Him in humility.

Are you looking for honor? Do you desire heavenly recognition? You will only discover these when you choose humility in your life.

Riches and Life

I do not believe in the philosophy of being true to God just so He will make me rich. However, I believe in His Word enough to know that there are certain promises He might choose to fulfill in my life. He will not do so because they are my goals, but He may choose to fulfill these promises because of His grace.

One of these promises relates to living a life of humility. The Bible says in Proverbs 22:4, "The reward of humility and the fear of the Lord are riches, honor, and life." When humility and reverence are our choices, God may choose to bless us with riches and life.

These riches may be eternal riches and this life may be eternal life. But these riches may be God's material supply to meet our needs on this earth and His desire to give us a meaningful and fulfilling life. My point is this: When you choose humility in your life, you never go wrong. The benefits are many. The rewards are great. Choosing humility is a choice toward God. A choice toward God always results in His blessings on our lives.

Choosing humility is a choice toward God. A choice toward God always results in His blessings on our lives.

Happiness

When Jesus washed the disciples' feet and told them His desire that they serve others, He also told them what would result in their lives if they did. "If you know these things, you are blessed if you do them" (John 13:17). He encouraged them to be humble and willing to serve others as a servant would serve his master. Jesus taught them that whenever they fulfilled these opportunities to be servants, He would bless them.

The word *blessed* means happy. Was Jesus telling them that a heart full of humility would result in happiness? Yes! To have a servant's spirit and a servant's heart will result in happiness.

Would you like to be happy in your life? Choose humility; it leads to happiness. This concept is alien to our society, but very familiar to Jesus Christ. Humility was His life. It was not an act or a duty to Him. It was the life that He chose as the Son of God.

Will you choose humility? Will you choose to be like the Lord Jesus Christ? Humility will bring power to your life—the kind of power that may bring honor, riches, life, and happiness to you.

Humility is a far better choice than pride. The results are greater. The blessings are superior. The power is Jesus' power!

SIX

Choosing Self-control

Self-control is tested in many different ways, but mine is tested most frequently when I am behind the wheel of my car. It may occur if I am running late for an appointment and it just so happens everyone in front of me is surveying the neighborhood at a very leisurely pace, or when traveling long distances and it just seems I am getting nowhere. When we are traveling as a family and stop for a moment, I always feel that it is imperative that I make up the lost time when the trip resumes. Driving makes me want to conquer all obstacles and arrive quickly at my destination.

Even though the tests of self-control come in different forms to each of us, we must realize that having self-control will always be a challenge in our lives. Making a choice to practice self-control is just the beginning of accepting that challenge. Problems, trouble, stress, and obstacles in our way all seem to undermine our resolve to choose self-control in our lives.

I guarantee that I struggle as much as anyone in this area. Years ago I began a spiritual practice that has helped me greatly maintain a self-controlled life. It all began when I was reading the Bible one day and noticed the following passage in Galatians 5:22–23: "But the fruit of the Spirit is love, joy, peace, patience, kindness, goodness, faithfulness, gentleness, self-control; against such things there is no law."

I realized, for the first time, that there is an association between the Holy Spirit and self-control. I learned through studying the passage that self-control is part of the spiritual fruit that grows as a result of being controlled by the Holy Spirit. Therefore, I began two practices.

First, I began to pray daily that I would be filled with the Holy Spirit. The word *filled* that is used in the New Testament means to be controlled. Therefore, I understood that I was either being controlled by the Holy Spirit or by my selfish will. When my will was in control, it meant my life was out of control. Being controlled by the Holy Spirit empowers me to practice self-control.

Through the years, I began to desire the Holy Spirit to control me moment by moment. As I begin my day with God, I practice surrendering my whole life to Him. I give Him my mind, will, emotions, spirit, body, tongue, attitude, motives, past, present, future, career, job, family, resources, and the various problems I am facing at the time. Upon surrendering each of these to the Lord, I ask the Holy Spirit to control my life. Upon receiving His control in my life, I am then able to live in self-control rather than live a life subject to chaos.

Secondly, I pray daily for all the events of my day I know I will face. As I share these with the Lord, I am prepared to have self-control during these various events. Therefore, I present to God each appointment or engagement. Anything I know I am going to face, I give it to the Lord, asking Him to give me self-control in each situation.

Am I always under the control of the Holy Spirit? No, but it is my desire to be. Do I ever give in to the temptation not to practice self-control? Yes, and when I do, I confess it to God as sin and receive His forgiveness in my life. It is a challenge to live a Spirit-controlled, self-controlled life.

There is a principle we need to learn: as we choose to be controlled by the Holy Spirit, we will experience greater self-control. Do you desire to be in control rather than out of control? The answer is to choose to be filled with the Holy Spirit. As this occurs, you will exemplify self-control in all situations. For each of us, this is a choice to have God's power in our lives.

As we choose to be controlled by the Holy Spirit, we will experience greater self-control.

Self-control: Consistency and Inconsistency

At times we seem to have total control, and then, in a brief moment, we lose it. Our temper flares, we speak a harsh word, or make a sarcastic remark. This lack of control seems to thwart our best efforts, often at the most crucial times. The life of Moses can teach us about consistency and inconsistency of self-control.

The Consistency of Self-control

God's call came to Moses while he was in the wilderness. God made it clear that He wanted Moses to lead His people out of Egyptian bondage. This was a tremendous spiritual and physical challenge for Moses. How was he going to lead two million plus people out of slavery into freedom? God had already told him that He was going to lead them into the promised land of Canaan He had prepared for them. As Moses surrendered to God's call, he successfully led the people out of the land of Egypt; however, this was only the beginning of his greatest challenge.

Moses' greatest challenge was serving as the leader of these ungrateful people. On many occasions Moses had to make the choice to stay in control rather than losing his patience with the people. It would have been so easy for him to do so.

A short time after the children of Israel departed from Egypt, Moses faced the crisis of the Red Sea. Behind him was the angry army of Pharaoh which had regrouped and was determined to take the Israelites back to Egypt. Before him was the Red Sea. Immediately the people began to harass Moses, complaining that he led them out of bondage only for them to be killed by Pharaoh's army.

Did he lose control and become impatient with them? No, because the Lord spoke to him, and in obedience to God's command, the Red Sea parted. The people began to cross on dry ground where the sea had been. What a miracle! As Pharaoh's army approached them in all its great might, the Lord rolled the waters back on them, destroying them. Moses' consistent control of himself led God's people to victory.

The people of God began to murmur against Moses' leadership again as they needed water and food. They accused him in anger of bringing them out into the wilderness only to die of starvation. They were relentless in their attacks upon Moses. Once again, the power of God granted them sufficient food and water. Moses' consistent calm in the crisis indicated his great strength. What a tremendous example this was for the people of God to see. This man of God was demonstrating a life of control as He trusted God and waited for His word to be given to him in the midst of every crisis.

Time after time Moses demonstrated self-control. Moses' godly choices were used to usher in the power of God on the children of Israel. On some occasions, God was ready to bring mighty judgment on these people, but stayed His hand because of the intervention of Moses. Moses' self-control is a great example to anyone who serves as a leader of people. There were so many times he could have easily lost his temper, but he chose a better way—self-control.

Consistency is important in our lives, especially when it is consistency in practicing self-control. It is very important that people who observe our lives from a distance see consistent self-control. I believe that even as Moses' self-control ushered in the power of God in his life, in the same way, God's power will be exercised in our lives when we consistently practice self-control. Self-control is a godly choice that leads to God's power.

The Inconsistency of Self-control

Since no person is perfect, we must also consider Moses' inconsistency in practicing self-control. Typically, he practiced self-control; however, there was at least one time he did not, and it resulted in a very catastrophic consequence for him.

The people were engaging in their daily gripe session against Moses. They were without water again and were asking him why he had brought them out to the wilderness to die of thirst. Moses' frustration level was building. How much longer could he put up with such negative, faithless remarks? How much longer could he be in control of these wretched people without losing his leadership? He was simply trying to obey the Lord.

Hearing the complaints, Moses and Aaron fell on their faces before the Lord. God spoke the following words to them; learn from this text how they responded to God's instruction:

"Take the rod; and you and your brother Aaron assemble the congregation and speak to the rock before their eyes, that it may yield its water. You shall thus bring forth water for them out of the rock and let the congregation and their beasts drink." So Moses took the rod from before the Lord, just as He had commanded him; and Moses and Aaron gathered the assembly before the rock. And he said to them, "Listen now, you rebels; shall we bring forth water for you out of this rock?" Then Moses lifted up his hand and struck the rock twice with his rod; and water came forth abundantly, and the congregation and their beasts drank. But the Lord said to Moses and Aaron, "Because you have not believed Me, to treat Me as holy in the sight of the sons of Israel, therefore you shall not bring this assembly into the land which I have given them." (Num. 20:8–12)

Moses' loss of self-control resulted in a great loss to himself and Aaron. God did provide the water, but told Moses and Aaron that they would not be allowed to lead the people into the promised land.

It is hard to understand why the consequence was so severe, especially after all they had endured. But since Moses was a leader, he was under a stricter standard than the others. He knew better than to disobey God. He did get water for the people, but he did not do it in the way God planned. The result was that he would never step foot in the promised land. For Moses, this brief lapse in self-control cost him everything for which he had worked so long as the leader of the people. God still used Moses in future days, probably in a greater way than before. Yet, he died before the people entered the promised land. God always does what He says He is going to do. You can always count on His Word.

When we demonstrate inconsistency in self-control, we experience not only the immediate negative result, but often we experience long-term negative consequences. If a parent loses self-control at the wrong time with his child, that child may bitterly remember the incident for years. If an employee or employer loses self-control, the consequences can be grave for business. Inconsistency in self-control can be a major problem in many ways. The consequences are never good, and are very often quite severe. A choice to lose control negates the intervention of God in your life.

According to Jesus, what we say comes straight out of what is in our hearts. Our words often demonstrate inconsistency in our self-control. Words are so powerful that we need to remember every day that "He who restrains his words has knowledge, and he who has a cool spirit is a man of understanding. Even a fool, when he keeps silent, is considered wise; when he closes his lips, he is counted prudent" (Prov. 17:27–28). If Moses had known of these words before he struck the rock, he could have led the people into the land of Canaan. Silence is wisdom. Knowing when to speak and when not to is prudence.

Since consistency in practicing self-control is so important, we need to know how to read the signals that we are losing control.

Five Signals of a Life Out of Control

You approach an intersection and the yellow light is flashing. What does this signal mean? The yellow light is a caution light. It means you need to look in all directions for traffic to enable you to travel on safely. Without the signal, you might go through the intersection without any hesitation.

I believe there are some obvious signals of a life going out of control. If one or more of these signals appear in your life, then you are living out of control. There are five signals that indicate a life out of control.

Spiritual Inconsistency

I have many opportunities to be around some of the most wonderful Christian leaders in America. I also meet people from all kinds of backgrounds. Some are pastors or staff members of churches, but most are laypersons who love the Lord and desire to serve Him.

When I visit with them privately, I discover that so many are living inconsistent spiritual lives. In fact, I meet pastors, staff members, and major church lay leaders who do not even have a consistent time with God every day. Out of seven days, many of them feel they have been pretty successful if they have a time with God on four of these days. With great intentions they come to me and ask how they can get in on the depths of God's power. They simply do not see a correlation between personal time with God and the experience of His power.

Spiritual inconsistency is a major problem among Christians. One proof of this is inconsistent church attendance; the best of us may be present only forty of fifty-two Sundays a year. Spiritual inconsistency is a reason why people are so reluctant to make a one-year leadership commitment in the church. Spiritual inconsistency is to blame for Christian families not surviving the attacks of Satan and many of them falling apart. Spiritual inconsistency is why so many churches are filled with division and strife rather than experiencing a mighty moving of God.

> *There is a correlation between self-control and spiritual consistency.*

It is important for you to understand that there is a correlation between self-control and spiritual consistency. Each one depends upon the other for spiritual success to result. Spiritual inconsistency is a signal that life is out of control.

Emotional Outbursts

When someone throws a temper tantrum, I have heard bystanders justify the action with: "You know that is just the way he is. Do not take it personally." Emotional outbursts are unacceptable to the Lord. They demonstrate a life out of control. Each of us needs to be responsible to others for the mistakes we make through our emotional outbursts.

An emotional outburst is a child reacting to a parental decision he may not agree with or appreciate. It is a wife exploding to her husband at the end of the day because her day at home or on her job did not go well. It is a father demonstrating anger to his children generated by the stress on his job. It is an executive walking out of a meeting yelling and screaming because the profit margin is not acceptable. An emotional outburst could also result when a church member who dislikes some direction of the church becomes inappropriately and overtly critical because the church is the only place this person gets to vent his frustrations about life. Whatever the cause, an emotional outburst indicates that life is out of control.

Have you ever seen an angry person deny she is angry when confronted about it? The more you talk to her, the angrier she becomes. People cannot live in denial of their emotional outbursts. We must face them as we face other problems. Tolerance only leads to deep wounds and hurts for those who are the target of our emotional tantrums.

When you choose to explode emotionally, you are not demonstrating self-control, part of the fruit of the Holy Spirit. Instead, self reigns alone in your life and the Holy Spirit is grieved and quenched. Here again, to choose self-control is to make a godly choice.

Lack of Discipline

A lack of discipline is another signal of a life out of control, and it can be detected in many ways: habitual tardiness, settling for mediocrity, sloppy dress, a loose tongue, ineffective crisis management, or an unhealthy body.

Since discipline results from training, we need to train ourselves to be under God's controlling Spirit so that self-control will be the spiritual result. There is no way we can selfishly maintain personal control. It is a product of the Holy Spirit. When it is present in our lives, there is discipline. When it is missing, a disciplined life will not occur. A choice for self-control is a choice for discipline.

Uncontrolled Tongue

When people cannot or will not control their tongues, they are not living a self-controlled life. The Bible says in James 3:2,

"For we all stumble in many ways. If anyone does not stumble in what he says, he is a perfect man, able to bridle the whole body as well." This verse indicates that when we control what we say, all of life is also in control. Conversely, as the rest of James 3 states, a tongue out of control is set on fire from hell (see v. 6). It is also indicative that self-control is not being practiced (see vv. 5–12).

An uncontrolled tongue causes turmoil in the family, in the business world, and in the church. A tongue out of control results in people being hurt and goals not being reached. An uncontrolled tongue never encourages anyone. It only tears down.

Choose self-control through the control of the Spirit in your life. When you do, the words you speak will demonstrate a life of control and order rather than disorder and chaos. We cannot control our words in our own strength. The Holy Spirit is needed to bring about such control.

Unhealthy Body

Everyone is sick at times, even when they are physically fit and eat a balanced diet. However, most sickness strikes people because they are not taking care of their bodies.

Exercise is important to physical fitness. When you are fit, you operate at a totally different level of endurance than when you are not.

For one year I have been faithfully working out at least five days a week. I never look forward to that thirty minutes of my day. In fact, once that thirty minutes is over, I feel I have conquered my biggest task of the day! When I made a commitment to exercise, it was a serious commitment. The result is a better attitude, a better outlook on life, and most of all, a more healthy body.

A proper diet is also very important to a healthy body. Since my wife's bout with cancer in 1990, we have changed our eating habits. We now feel better.

A body out of control indicates that your life is out of control. It takes self-control to exercise consistently and to eat properly. Choose self-control for your life. I believe you will live longer if you do.

Each of these signals—spiritual inconsistency, emotional outbursts, a lack of discipline, an uncontrolled tongue, and an unhealthy body—can be indicators that you are living a life out of control.

Certain signals can be indicators that you are living a life out of control.

Are there any consequences to living a life out of control? Yes! The Bible speaks about these very clearly.

Consequences of Having No Self-control

There are many consequences of lacking self-control. In concluding this chapter, I want to highlight four of these consequences clearly taught in the Word of God.

Vulnerability to Attack

What is vulnerability? When you have no self-control in your life, you are opening yourself to attack and allowing potential damage to be done either emotionally or physically, if not both.

The Bible descriptively teaches, "Like a city that is broken into and without walls, Is a man who has no control over his spirit" (Prov. 25:28).

In ancient times, the walls of a city indicated security and power. When a city had breaches in its wall, these openings allowed its safety to be threatened by attacks from its enemies. This is what a person does when he has no control over his spirit. He opens himself to attack from enemies without and within, and ultimately, to attack from the enemy Satan. A life out of control is terribly vulnerable.

When you do not choose self-control, you are inviting the spiritual attacks of Satan against your life. He attacks you at the point of your weaknesses and renders you virtually helpless. His fierceness becomes greater when you are out of control.

> *When self-control is lost, it is like putting down weapons and surrendering to the power of an enemy.*

This is why families lose the battle so often. This is why churches are in controversy. This is why our nation is weak morally. This is why the corporate world is filled with greed. When self-control is lost, it is like putting down weapons and surrendering to the power of an enemy. Defeat is inevitable and imminent.

Anger

Anger always results from a lack of self-control. An angry person cannot live a life under God's control bearing the fruit of self-control. Anger creates a life of selfishness, revenge, carelessness, and chaos.

The Bible speaks about anger in many places. Notice that it says, "An angry man stirs up strife, and a hot-tempered man abounds in transgression" (Prov. 29:22). Factions and divisions are results of anger. When anyone loses control of his temper, he sins. Anger is a sin. It is a terrible consequence of living without control. Again, the Bible speaks about anger, "A gentle answer turns away wrath, but a harsh word stirs up anger" (Prov. 15:1).

When we respond with gentleness in a difficult situation, the result can be totally different than when we respond with a harsh word. Anger is stirred up by harsh words. Harsh words are spoken when life is not in control.

Anger leads to family disruptions and divisions. Anger leads to cliques in business. Anger leads to splits in churches. There is nothing good about anger. It is a tragic consequence of a life out of control.

Conflict

Conflict destroys families, churches, businesses, and even countries. Conflict is a terrible consequence of a life out of control. In Proverbs 29:22, we learned that strife or conflict is the result of an angry, out-of-control person.

World wars have occurred because certain people were not self-controlled. They were nothing more than loose guns in a shaky environment. Marriages have ended after many years because of unresolved conflict. Two out-of-control people married to each other are a potential explosion.

Many times pastors and church members do not get along because self-control is lacking. Conflict distracts many churches from the mission of touching the world with the gospel message.

Conflict is evident in so many segments of our society today. Is there an answer? Yes! The answer is to be controlled by the Holy Spirit which always results in the fruit of self-control.

Abounding Sins

Have you ever started your day out wonderfully? Then something hits you the wrong way. You fly off the handle. Your spouse becomes angry, your children are disappointed, and your day is ruined.

This is what I mean by abounding sins. The Bible says in Proverbs 29:22 that a hot temper leads to many sins. Losing control in your life is never good. It makes you vulnerable to the attacks of Satan which always leads to more sin in your life.

These abounding sins come in many forms, but once the first defense falls, a domino effect occurs. Abounding sins absolutely devastate your life; and they begin when you lose control at one point in your life.

The consequences of having no self-control are many—I have highlighted only four. What makes the consequences different? The answer is in the choices you make in your life.

When you choose to be godly, you will desire to live a life controlled by the Holy Spirit, a life that always bears the fruit of self-control. This is a choice for God's power to flow through your life. It is a much better choice than anything your selfishness can offer you.

Choosing self-control is a God-honoring choice! Choosing self-control is a right choice! Choosing self-control is a smart choice! Choosing self-control is a power choice—a choice to experience God's power in your life!

Choosing Pure Motives

There is a leadership crisis in America that could jeopardize the future of our nation. When a nation loses its values, morals erode and the nation degenerates toward self-destruction. Where does this leadership crisis exist?

It exists in the political arena. What is expedient has become more important than what is right. The people of America do not know what or who to believe about the condition of our nation. Truth is shaded, actions of mischief are winked at, and compromise is applauded. If the future of our nation depends on its leaders, where are those who will pull us out of this leadership vacuum in our country?

This leadership crisis also exists in the world of business. Corporate leaders are summarily dismissed when the growth of a company does not meet the expectations of the corporation's board. It is no longer enough to simply make a profit; there must be larger and larger profits each year. The world of business is also not very family friendly. Many companies expect employees to make their careers their primary focus or move over for someone who will. It is apparent that values are being compromised, and fueled by greed and are being replaced by temporal things like concern for profit only.

This leadership crisis also exists in the religious world. Fidelity to biblical truth is being exchanged for convenience and comfort. A life above reproach has been exchanged for a life of luxury and pleasure. Many preachers are far more political than prophetic. Exaggerated claims are accepted as the norm instead of being viewed as sin. The passion of many religious leaders is no longer to change but to put change in their pockets. The disparity between the public and private lives of many of them is appalling. Where are the prophets who will stand for biblical truth, proclaim it, and live it with courage before the world?

When I think about the leadership crisis in our nation, it makes me ask, "Where are the real leaders?" How many are there to whom the world listens with confidence when they speak? Are there leaders who have such credibility that, when they speak, the whole world listens? Are there leaders with high moral and ethical credentials anywhere in politics, business, or religion?

Could this leadership crisis exist because of questionable motives in the lives of those who aspire to lead? Where are the leaders who have pure motives, who are more interested in what is right and what is best for others than in what is politically expedient and right for them? Only leaders who lead with pure motives will be the ones to change the world for the better.

Pure motives will exist in leaders who have the courage to stand for what is right. What is right is what God says, not what people think. What is right is what God wants, not what we desire. The kind of leaders who will lead people toward what is right in the eyes of God will be courageous leaders indeed.

Pure motives will exist in leaders who have integrity in their personal, private, and public lives. The world is crying for men and women who will lead with integrity, who will follow through on their word all the way to the end.

The leaders of this world must be known for a passion to change the world. We need world changers, not world conformers, leading in political, business, and religious arenas. Whenever you have a chance to vote leaders into office, work for leaders on the job, or elect leaders in the church, make certain they are world changers—the kinds of leaders controlled by courage, integrity, and passion.

Pure motives are often lacking in the world today, both in the lives of leaders, and in the lives of everyday people. Many have only a personal agenda, rather than the right agenda—changing the world by doing what is right in God's eyes.

Our motives are determined by what is in our heart. We cannot determine the motives of someone else's heart. God alone knows. If there is a problem with a person's motives, there is a problem with the heart. Therefore, look with me to the problem.

The Problem of the Heart

The greatest barrier to having pure motives is sinfulness of the human heart. The heart is very deceptive. In fact, the Bible says in Jeremiah 17:9, "The heart is more deceitful than all else and is desperately sick; who can understand it?"

The sinfulness of the human heart shows in the choices we make. In Proverbs 21:2 we read, "Every man's way is right in his own eyes, but the Lord weighs the heart."

When we are making a choice, we have to be careful that we do not attempt to justify our choice. At times we make a choice which seems to be right; however, due to sinfulness in our heart, our perspective is not the same as God's.

We learn from the teachings of Jesus that our words reflect what is in the heart. The Bible says in Matthew 12:33–35,

> Either make the tree good, and its fruit good; or make the tree rotten, and its fruit rotten; for the tree is known by its fruit. You brood of vipers, how can you, being evil, speak what is good? For the mouth speaks out of that which fills the heart. The good man out of his good treasure brings forth what is good; and the evil man out of his evil treasure brings forth what is evil.

Through our lives we demonstrate whether our heart is right or our heart is evil. If the heart is evil, the words that are spoken will be evil. Jesus says that our heart—and our motives—needs to be pure in order for our lives to demonstrate goodness.

God's power must fill our hearts if we are going to choose pure motives in our lives.

The challenge before us is to adhere to Jesus' teaching to overcome the deceitfulness of the heart. Only God has the power to know what is in our heart, and He alone is able to weigh our motives. Right choices are possible when the heart is pure and devoted to God. He is powerful enough to overcome the deceitfulness of the human heart. God's power must fill our hearts if we are going to choose pure motives in our lives.

The Source of Pure Motives

According to the Bible, God instructed Samuel to seek out and anoint the man chosen to succeed King Saul. The Lord told Samuel to go to Bethlehem to the house of Jesse, for it would be through this family that the next king would come.

The sons of Jesse were paraded before Samuel for him to determine which one was to be anointed king. After the sons were brought before him, Samuel did not sense God's leadership to anoint any of them. He asked Jesse if he had any other sons, and Jesse replied that he had one other, the youngest, out tending the sheep. When this young man was brought before Samuel, it was immediately evident to him that this one, David, was to be the king. Samuel anointed David as the next king of Israel.

Why was David chosen? He was the youngest of them and a mere shepherd. His older brothers appeared to be better suited for the job. But God does not look on outward appearances; instead, He examines the condition of the heart.

Therefore, we would do well to search for the qualities that were found in David's heart. When we discover these qualities, we will learn why the Lord chose David to be Israel's king. Examine with me the kind of heart David had.

A Willing Heart

One of the qualities of David's heart was his willingness to honor God. The Bible records this willingness in Acts 13:22. "And after He had removed him, He raised up David to be their king, concerning whom He also testified and said, 'I have found David the son of Jesse, *a man after My heart*, who will do all My will'" (emphasis added).

David was known for being a man after God's own heart, a man with great devotion to the Lord.

What does this tell us about David? It means he was willing to do the will of God in all circumstances. He was so devoted to the Lord that God knew he preferred His will over his own. David had a willing heart. This is one of the reasons God anointed him to be the king of Israel.

David's motives were pure because of his willingness to do the will of God. He chose pure motives rather than his own selfish will. If there was a conflict between his will and the will of God, God knew David's intent was to obey Him.

If we are going to choose pure motives in our lives, we need to have a willing heart. Our prayer everyday needs to be, "Lord,

I want to be a person after Your heart, willing to do all of Your will." This prayer will nurture a willing heart in our lives. That will help us to choose pure motives.

I have found that a person will never be anointed for greatness unless his heart is willing to do all of God's will.

How willing are you to do God's will? What if He led you to do something you preferred not to do? What if He led you away from your place of comfort to a totally unfamiliar environment? I have found that a person will never be anointed for greatness unless his heart is willing to do all of God's will.

A person does not have to hang a billboard around his neck that says, "I am willing to do God's will." You may be a "no name" in your profession, but if you are willing to do God's will, He will find you. God has your heart's telephone number. He will always remember the person who is willing to do all of His will. A willing heart is essential to having pure motives.

A Right Heart

David had a right heart before God. The Bible says in Psalm 78:70–72, "He also chose David His servant, and took him from the sheepfolds; from the care of the ewes with suckling lambs He brought him, to shepherd Jacob His people, and Israel His inheritance. So he shepherded them according to the integrity of his heart, and guided them with his skillful hands."

What kind of shepherd was David? Even though others saw David's job as insignificant, he performed it as though it was the most important job in the world. I have always felt the same about every place God has called me to minister. I always felt that each was the greatest opportunity in the world, places where I could touch the world for Jesus Christ.

So many people are not content with their lives. They believe Satan's lie that the grass is always greener on the other side of the fence—another job, a different spouse, a smaller town. It is good to remember that people who live "on the other side of the fence" usually see the grass as brown rather than green. We must understand the value of making the best of where we are in life. The old saying, "Bloom where you are planted," is very applicable to the person with a right heart. God will determine where you are in the future; you are to give your all wherever you are located.

If you are going to choose pure motives, you need to have a right heart, one that is not only willing to do all of God's will, but also believes your job or calling in life is the most important thing you could ever do. If you perform your present job well, the Lord may then determine that He wants to entrust you with another task in life.

The most important place to be is in the center of God's will. This is your place of safety and success. Whatever God's will is for you is not insignificant or unimportant. You must operate your life out of pure motives. Pure motives will motivate you to do all you can wherever you are and realize it is up to God whether you do anything else somewhere else.

A Prepared Heart

The Bible says in Psalm 78:72 that David led the flock of sheep with skillful hands. This means that he led them with insight, intelligence, and wisdom. When David was combining his skillfulness with his personal belief that he was living out God's greatest calling as a shepherd, God was preparing him for something far greater later. The things he learned in shepherding prepared him to lead the people of God as their king. His fathers and his brothers saw a shepherd boy, but God saw a king!

God will never lead you to do something else unless He has prepared you. The Lord's business is placing His people in the right places. He determines where we spend our lives and He will not misplace you. God does not make mistakes. He will only lead you to another place after he has prepared you for it. Just as he did with David, He will do with you. He will prepare you for a new place of service through your present place of service.

There are no shortcuts with God. He will never use a person in a major way unless that person is prepared. Moses was in the desert forty years before God used him to lead His people out of Egypt. Jesus was prepared for thirty years before His ministry went public for three years.

When God discovers a man, woman, or young person whose heart is willing, right, and prepared, He may choose that person for extraordinary greatness.

You have worth as a person! What you are doing at the present time has worth if it is the will of God for you. Do not listen to voices who would tell you it is not important! God wants to take you from where you are and develop you fully in order to prepare to use you in a greater way.

If you have a prepared heart, your opportunities will be great. When preparation meets opportunity, a divine appointment for your life is kept. Conversely, if you are not prepared in your life, your opportunities will be limited.

A choice to have pure motives must involve your taking seriously what you are presently doing. You need to do whatever you do with insight, intelligence, and wisdom. Your prepared heart will catch the attention of the Lord.

David was passed over by his own father and brothers as being king material. However, God did not pass him by. Why? God always looks upon the heart. David's heart was willing, right, and prepared. God was impressed with his heart; therefore, He chose to use him in a great way.

The source of pure motives is the heart. When God discovers a man, woman, or young person whose heart is willing, right, and prepared, He may choose that person for extraordinary greatness.

Before God chooses us for greatness, we need to make some right choices—choices of the heart, choices that result from pure motives. These choices are daily choices, important choices, choices that make God's power real to us.

Checking Your Motives

Periodically, I have the opportunity to fly in a private airplane. It always intrigues me to watch the pilot prepare for the flight. He follows a checklist that provides a list of things to do before he gets the aircraft in the air. Any smart pilot will make certain he has gone through this list. He will not assume that he remembers to do the things on the list or that his aircraft passes all of the checks. Following the checklist assures him, as much as is possible, that his aircraft is ready for flight. He can then expect his journey to be completed safely.

I believe there is a checklist to help you determine your motives that you need to go through daily. It is important, just like a pilot, that we never assume our preparedness or be inconsistent in our adherence to it. We must faithfully check our motives by this list. There are three questions we can ask ourselves daily because perhaps the answers will unveil the real motives that exist in our hearts.

Am I Living by the Principles of the Word of God?

I believe the Bible is the Word of God. I believe it is to be our authority for living, including decision making. As I recognize its authority over my life, then I refuse to compromise its teachings and principles for living.

If I am ready to check my motives, I should begin with the question, "Am I living by the principles of the Word of God?" This question forces me to deal with an important issue—the impact that the Word of God has on my decisions.

Jill had been dating Bill for about two years. Bill surprised her Valentine's Day with an engagement ring. In a very romantic setting, he proposed. Jill agreed immediately to marry him.

When she told her parents, they did not share in her joy. Jill and her parents were born-again Christians and committed to the Word of God. They were never in favor of Jill's dating Bill, much less marrying him. They asked Jill to evaluate her motives, to ask herself honestly why she wanted to marry Bill.

Jill took their challenge and began to ask herself the question, "Am I living by the principles of the Word of God in this decision?" For the first time in her life, she finally understood it was not right for her to date or marry Bill because he was an unbeliever. The Holy Spirit brought genuine conviction. She was heart-broken because she loved Bill. However, she also loved the Lord and His Word and knew she should not compromise this area of her life.

After sharing her discovery with her parents, they were happy with her decision. Their prayers had been answered, but they also felt the pain she faced in telling Bill. However, they knew God would honor her for being true to the principles of His Word. Jill, with a broken and repentant heart, ended the engagement with Bill and told him why she had to make this decision.

A couple of years later, Jill met a young man named David. He was an outstanding young Christian. They prayed on dates. They shared what God wanted to do in each of their lives. In time, they fell in love, became engaged, and eventually married. Today they are serving the Lord in a great way.

If Jill had not been willing to ask herself a terribly difficult question and to yield her will to God's, she would have made the greatest mistake of her life. She chose, however, to call herself to accountability to the Word of God. It does not matter how a person rationalizes or justifies a decision; there is no reason for ever compromising a principle of the Word of God.

Read the Bible daily. Learn the principles of His Word by which He wants you to live. Make a commitment in your heart that God's Word is going to be your authority. Then ask yourself regularly, "Am I living by the principles of the Word of God?" If you can answer with a resounding "Yes," then your motive is pure. If you cannot answer in the affirmative, then it is not. Choose God's way, the way of the Word. You can never go wrong in this choice.

Is My Spirit Right?

It is important that a person is not just committed to doing the right thing, but to doing the right thing in the right way. This means doing it with the right spirit.

I heard years ago, "If the devil cannot get you to do the wrong thing, he will get you to do the right thing in the wrong way." Those of us really committed to the Word of God need to seriously check our spirit regularly. We need to ask ourselves, "Is my spirit right?"

When we stand before society upholding the principles of God's Word, let us never be guilty of standing for them with the wrong spirit. We can lose our witness to a secular society if we have the spirit of the Pharisees of Jesus' day. They lived by their countless rules, but their spirits were caustic and offensive. We need to have the spirit of love bathe our lives so that people can see Jesus through us.

Am I Placing Others Before Myself?

Any person who places his or her personal desires and goals before everyone and everything else is guilty of having wrong motives. We must have the humility of Jesus who placed the welfare of others before His own. Others are to be more important than our own agendas in life.

Jesus taught His disciples that those who want to be first will be last, and those who are willing to be last will be first. This is the reason for the question, " Am I placing others before myself?"

As I make decisions about my life and ministry, I really need to be willing to ask myself this question. Am I doing this for me or for others? We must be willing to ask ourselves hard questions, the kind of questions that help us check our motives.

Even as the pilot makes his way to the runway, he is checking off his list to prepare the aircraft for flight. He will abandon the flight if the checklist cannot be completed perfectly.

"Am I living my life by the principles of God's Word?"
"Is my spirit right?"
"Am I placing others before myself?"

In the same way, we need to check our motives in everything we do. What we do is not as important as why we do it. We need to ask ourselves: "Am I living my life by the principles of God's Word?" "Is my spirit right?" "Am I placing others before myself?" If we get positive answers, then chances are our motives are pure.

What a great challenge to choose right motives in life! It is difficult due to the natural deceitfulness of the heart, but not impossible by the power of God.

A checklist such as this is needed to solve and overcome the leadership crisis in America. Political, business, and church leaders today need to take an honest look at who they are. They need to be willing to ask the difficult questions of themselves and their colleagues. Perhaps this would begin to solve the leadership crisis so that the people of this land will once again be able to place their confidence in the leadership of this country.

❧

PART THREE

Choices
to Real Success

CHOOSING GOD'S WILL

CHOOSING GOD'S PROSPERITY

CHOOSING ACCOUNTABILITY

CHOOSING SPIRITUAL VICTORY

E I G H T

Choosing God's Will

He was intrigued and fascinated with great wealth. Leaving his family and friends, he began his search for a mine of diamonds. Although he was a successful farmer, he left this profession hoping he would quickly find his fortune. He did not discover diamonds. In the end, unable to bear his failure, he fell to his death in the sea. His name was Ali Hafed, the character in Russell H. Conwell's book, *Acres of Diamonds*.

The story, however, does not end with the death of Hafed, it continues with the man who bought Ali's farm. As he was working one day on his newly acquired land, he discovered a large black stone. Impressed with its texture and shape, he displayed it in his home as a keepsake.

One day a friend was visiting and noticed the stone. He thought Ali Hafed must have returned with a diamond from his worldwide search for wealth. The man who bought Hafed's farm explained to the friend that he had discovered it in his backyard while working the land.

His friend felt that the stone could be valuable, so the two men went to the backyard to dig and came across hundreds of stones much like the first. Upon closer inspection, these stones proved to be diamonds. The farm became one of the great diamond mines in the world.

Think how Ali Hafed's life would have been different had he chosen to begin his search for diamonds in his own backyard. Hafed's wrong choice led to despair and death. He could not live with his failure to find wealth. One bad choice led to another. He ended his life when his search seemed futile. What a shame.

> *When we begin to understand that God is not playing "hide and seek" with His will, we will be able to trust Him more perfectly with what He is doing in our lives.*

There are Christians who search for the will of God all over the world, just like Hafed searched for diamonds. The tragedy is that many come to the same end. They are frustrated with the futility of their quest. They search for the will of God, yet the will of God is with them where they are in life. God does not hide His will from His children.

As a father, I would never taunt my children into guessing what I wanted them to do. In fact, the more important the task, the more committed I am to making my will or desire very clear to them. Children would not long trust a father who continually plays a guessing game with them. However, they will trust a father who clarifies his desires and direction for his children.

When we begin to understand that God is not playing "hide and seek" with His will, we will be able to trust Him more perfectly with what He is doing in our lives. When I make the choice in life to live in the will of God, the Father is pleased. He is going to do all He can to make His will plain to me.

Our desire should be to discover what God is doing around us. What is the activity of God going on nearest us? God's will is for us to join Him in what He is doing around us. If God is moving in an obvious manner around me, then I have no choice but to join Him. That is God's will for me.

For you to choose God's will for your life is for you to join the Lord in whatever He is doing in your world. I am not to sit on the sidelines with the skeptic or cynic who is critical of what God may be doing. His work is always obvious. When I join him, He will then begin to do His will through me.

I realize this may be an oversimplification of how to find God's will. I will be the first to admit that talking about God's will is far easier than discerning. When you are really trying to know the will of God, especially in an area of your life that will affect all the people in your life, it can be a real struggle.

The challenge is sometimes exaggerated. The challenge is not for you to know the will of God for one year from now, but it is for you to know the will of God today. Our commitment must be to live in the will of God daily. One day at a time should be our goal for living in God's will. Even as you go through the day, your challenge is to choose the will of God step by step and moment by moment. Do not let Satan or others worry you or stress you out about the distant future. The future is in God's hands. Your responsibility right now is to find out what He is doing around you today and then join Him in that—not for tomorrow, but for today.

Discovering the will of God, especially in a major area of your life, is sometimes a process. Before the Lord can clearly make His will known, He has to take you through a process of preparing you to do His will and bringing needed adjustments to your life. You should never let anyone push you into a choice concerning the will of God, for it is only when He has prepared you that His will may be made crystal clear to you.

It is a lot easier to understand the process I am describing when you look back at various decisions you have made in your life and recognize them as undoubtedly correct choices concerning the will of God. As you reflect on many of these decisions, you will discover those points of adjustment that you made in your thinking or your life which enabled you to do the will of God. Also, you will see that if you had felt immediate action was necessary either you would not have acted or perhaps done the wrong thing. There is a process He uses that enables you to know and eventually do His will.

God does not force His will upon you. However, as God guides you, He will help you discover His will through a process that may be filled with many points of adjustment. When you look back over the process, you will see how it helped you learn what God was doing and prepared you to join Him in that cause.

A Personal Testimony

Before I came to First Baptist Church, Springdale, Arkansas, I was serving a church in Texas as pastor. God was moving in a mighty way with many people coming to Christ. The church was experiencing its greatest days of growth. The movement of the Spirit was evident.

As in any church, when the Lord moves in a mighty way, the warfare can become rather tough. We had seen demonstrations of the mighty grace of God. However, we also had seen the attack of the evil one in a major way. Without any doubt, regardless of the warfare, I was convinced that God wanted me to be in that church as pastor. I had completed just over two and a half years as pastor of that church.

In the month of May that same year, I received a call from a staff member of First Baptist in Springdale, asking me if I would be interested in becoming the pastor of their church. He told me that the current pastor, who had sixteen years of wonderful success there, was going into an itinerant ministry, and the church was beginning their search for his successor.

I immediately told this staff member that I had no interest in coming to the church. I shared with him how God was moving in our fellowship and how I did not feel I could leave at that time. I thanked him for his confidence in me, especially since we had never met.

When I attended the Southern Baptist Convention in Atlanta that June, I was approached by a pastor I love and greatly respect. He told me that he had felt led of God to recommend me to a church in Arkansas. You guessed it—the First Baptist Church of Springdale. I was shocked. I began to wonder if God was going to do something new in our lives. My wife had already told me that she felt God was going to move us to a new ministry soon. I trusted her spiritual walk but was not convinced it was time for the Lord to do something.

When flying home from Atlanta, I was reading Charles Stanley's book, *How to Listen to God.* God began to create within me a spiritual restlessness, and by the time I arrived home I was convinced that indeed the Lord was going to make a change in our lives. I just did not know where He was going to lead us.

One morning in late July as I was praying, I felt led of God to write down five things which, as a pastor, I would want in the next church. When these things were crystal clear to me, I prayed about them and left the matter with the Lord.

In August, I was trying to fill a staff position in our church and was seeking recommendations. A name had come to my attention of a staff member of the First Baptist Church of Springdale. Since his church was without a pastor, I thought he might be interested in our position. As we spoke by telephone, he asked me why I did not have an interest in his church. I shared with him the process that God had taken me through and that I was willing to do whatever God wanted me to do.

At home later that day, I received a call from the chairman of the Pastor Search Committee in Springdale. Gene Layman, one of the godliest men I have ever known, shared with me the desire of his committee to come and talk with me. I gave them permission to do so, since God had obviously been trying to do something in my life since May of that year.

They came to hear me on the third Sunday of August. After meeting with me, our conversations continued. They came back on the second Sunday of September. They asked me to come and look over their situation, meet with their staff, and together make a final decision concerning the will of God. I came in view of a call to their church on the last Sunday of September. The church affirmed God's will which we had come to know in our hearts. On the last Sunday of October in that year, I became the senior pastor of the First Baptist Church, Springdale, Arkansas.

As I reflect on this decision, I see the process. God was moving in the situation on many occasions. This is what caught my attention. There were points of adjustment that were made in my life, in the church that I was serving at the time, and also in the life of the First Baptist Church of Springdale.

God is sovereign! He is in absolute control. When I choose to do the will of God, I have to be able to sense what He is doing around me. When I was in the middle of this process, I was not as keen spiritually as I should have been. Looking back, I now know that I and others affected by my move needed to go through this process so that God's will would be made clear to all involved.

Choosing God's will in life is a choice to real success. At times it is also a struggle. If your heart is right and you want His will for your life, He will make it known to you in His time. His timing usually involves a process in your life of getting you ready to recognize and do His will for your life.

The Prerequisite to the Will of God

The late Dr. George W. Truett, pastor of the First Baptist Church of Dallas, Texas, was known for the classic statement about the will of God. "Life's greatest discovery is knowing the will of God, but life's greatest accomplishment is doing the will of God.[1]"

Remember, though, there is a prerequisite to discovering the will of God for our lives .

Jesus understood the will of God better than anyone. He spent His life on earth in continual fellowship with His Father in order that He might do the will of His Father. Teaching in the temple one day, He spoke the following words concerning the will of God: "If any man is willing to do His will, he shall know of the teaching, whether it is of God, or whether I speak from Myself" (John 7:17). When Jesus said we would "know of the teaching," He was using the word *know* to mean "in an experiential manner."

The prerequisite to knowing the will of God in our lives is that we must be willing to do His will, whatever it may be. Until we are willing, we will not experience it. I believe that Jesus was saying to us, "Why should I manifest My will to you when I know already you are not willing to do it?"

> *There are two words that must never be used together in the life of a Christian. Those two words are, "No, Lord."*

There are two words that must never be used together in the life of a Christian. Those two words are, "No, Lord." When He is Lord, you have no choice but to do His will. The attitude of willingness needs to be so dominant that we periodically say, "Lord, whatever you want me to do, the answer is yes!"

Since this is a prerequisite to knowing the will of God, the question we need to always ask someone seeking God's will is, "Are you ready to do God's will?" If I need to know the mind of Christ about a matter, I must ask myself, "Am I ready to do God's will?" If we are not ready to do God's will, whatever it is, wherever it is, then all else about God's will is meaningless.

Therefore, we need to totally surrender ourselves daily to God. As we surrender wholly to God, then we will be willing and ready to do whatever He wants us to do. The result will be that God will reveal His will to us. Is there anything else that will be helpful to us as we desire to live in the will of God?

Three Key Words to Remember

The Bible gives some outstanding advice to us about the will of God. In Isaiah 55:8–9 we read, "'For My thoughts are not your thoughts, neither are your ways My ways,' declares the Lord. 'For as the heavens are higher than the earth, so are My ways higher than your ways, and My thoughts than your thoughts.'"

It is important to know that God's thoughts and ways are higher than ours. What He has in mind for us is always beyond what we dream for ourselves. Therefore, our challenge is to comprehend the level of God's ways and thoughts. When we do this, we will be more capable of living in the will of God.

Most Christians want to know the will of God. Many may not want to live it, but most desire to know it. Three key words need to guide all decision-making in the Christian's life.

Initiative

It is easy to manipulate circumstances in our lives. As Christians, we are tempted not only to manipulate them, but to say the Lord did it. This attitude is wrong and unacceptable.

Jesus said, concerning this subject:

> "Truly, truly, I say to you, the Son can do nothing of Himself, unless it is something He sees the Father doing; for whatever the Father does, these things the Son also does in like manner. For the Father loves the Son, and shows Him all things that He Himself is doing; and greater works than these will He show Him, that you may marvel." (John 5:19–20)

The Father initiated the work that He wanted Jesus to do in His life. Jesus only did what He saw the Father doing. As the Father initiated it, Jesus joined Him in it. This was possible because of their intimate relationship with one another.

As you have an intimate relationship with Jesus Christ, you will be able to see what God is doing around you. As you discern the activity of God taking place, it is important that you adjust your life and plans to what He is doing.

In all the decisions of your life, you need to ask, "Did God initiate this?" If God initiated it, then you need to pay attention to what He is doing. If you manipulated the circumstances, disregard it as not being the will of God. By having an intimate relationship with Jesus Christ, you will be able to understand God's activity as it begins to take place because He has chosen to take the initiative in the circumstances around you.

Timing

Sometimes I hear young men describe special women they have met. They tell me that even on their first date, they believed God was telling them that they were going to marry these girls. I usually tell these men that the time for them to get married is not now, but later when those girls come to the same decision.

In decision making, we move our understanding of God's will to another level. We begin by asking, "Did God initiate it?" This question must be followed by another, "Is it God's timing?" There are experiences when God may initiate activity in a situation and you think it is His will for your life. If indeed it is His will, the timing will also be perfect. Something can be good and godly, but the timing may not be right for it to take place. The Bible says in Ecclesiastes 3:1, 11, and 14:

There are experiences when God may initiate activity in a situation and you think it is His will for your life.

There is an appointed time for everything. And there is a time for every event under heaven . . . He had made everything appropriate in its time . . . I know that everything God does will remain forever; there is nothing to add to it and there is nothing to take from it, for God has so worked that men should fear him.

The timing is perfect if it is God's timing. His timing is evident because it makes us respect God for who He is. Out of our reverence for Him, we respect His timing, knowing that it is a key ingredient in relation to the will of God.

God is never too early. God is never too late. God is always on time. God has a timetable, and it is usually different than ours. Our challenge is to discern God's timetable in the decisions we make in our lives.

Submission

To choose God's will we must submit our will to His. The Bible says in Proverbs 3:5–6, "Trust in the Lord with all your heart, and do not lean on your own understanding. In all your ways acknowledge Him, and He will make your paths straight."

Our trust is only to be in the Lord. We are not to rely on our own understanding. As we submit our will to His will, the Lord clears the obstacles so that we are able to live out His will.

Initiative. Timing. Submission. These words are critical in relationship to the will of God. When you give careful attention to these three key ingredients in your search for God's will, you will experience real success in your life. Real success is choosing God's will for your life.

Three Positive Results of Living in God's Will

When you choose to live in the will of God every day, you will experience many positive results. I want to highlight three.

Continual Confidence

Choosing God's will for your life can give you confidence in your life. This is possible because your trust is in the Lord. When you place all your trust in the Lord, you can have the confidence that God will have His way and will help you rest in whatever happens. This confidence is real because you know God has been involved in determining what happens in your life.

The Bible addresses this again in Proverbs 16:33: "The lot is cast into the lap, but its every decision is from the Lord." In various situations in life, people may determine by chance what they should do. Proverbs teaches us that even decisions that are made by chance are decisions from the Lord.

When you accept God's will for your life, you can live with full confidence. God is going to have His way in your life when you make decisions based on His initiative, His timing, and your submission to what He is doing around you. In Romans 8:31 we read, "If God is for us, who is against us?"

This is confidence in the Lord. If we choose to do God's will in God's way, we will experience confidence in the Lord.

Continual Direction

What a joy it is to know that choosing the will of God will result in His continual direction of our lives. We no longer have to live in darkness, for His will provides the light for us. He makes the paths clear. He unveils the future to us one day at a time.

There are times I fear that I am getting ahead of the Lord in a given situation. Then I remember Proverbs 16:9: "The mind of man plans his way, but the Lord directs His steps."

I can attempt to calculate what God is going to do in my life; however, I cannot limit Him with my human calculations. I must be aware that I can attempt to plan my life, but only the Lord directs my steps. This not only gives me confidence, but guarantees me direction from the Lord.

This is verified in Proverbs 20:24: "Men's steps are ordained by the Lord. How then can man understand his way?" These God-given steps in our lives make us aware that we cannot understand our own ways. This is good for us to understand because the Lord is involved in every step we take in life.

There are many times we may not understand what God is doing. We may not be sure what He wants us to do. However, when we make the choice to do God's will we can be sure that God is directing and guiding our lives.

Continual Blessings

The continual blessings of God are yours when you choose to do the will of God. In fact, Deuteronomy 28:2 reminds us, "And all these blessings shall come upon you and overtake you, if you will obey the Lord your God."

The Lord pronounces multiple blessings upon those who will obey Him or choose to do His will. The rest of Deuteronomy 8 lists the various blessings that belong to the person who obeys God. These blessings may be in relationships, resources, and even upon your country. A choice to do God's will is a choice that will result in continual blessings in your life.

When a child obeys his parents, he will be blessed if the parents love him. If he becomes disobedient they may withhold their blessing. They may still love him, but their full blessings may not be granted if he continually chooses disobedience.

We are all blessed by the Lord. The Father bestows extraordinary blessings on those who will choose His will. The Bible is full of promises in regard to His blessings which follow our obedience to His will for our lives.

Do not worry about next week or next year, but live in the will of God today

When we make the right choice to experience real success in life, it is a choice that demands we choose God's will. When we are ready to do God's will and to discern His moving through His initiative and His timing, we will submit our will to the will of God. This entire action will result in giving us a continual confidence and a continual direction, and bestow upon us the continual blessings of God.

Look around you. Is God moving? Join Him in what He is doing. This is living in the will of God. Do not worry about next week or next year, but live in the will of God today. Do not search for God's will as a child would search for a hidden object. He is not hiding it from you. Discover what He is doing. Join Him in it. This is God's will for your life. God is in control. He ordains your steps. He determines the blessings upon your life.

Just think, all of this begins with a choice. A choice to do God's will. Choose real success. Choose God's will.

❧

NINE

Choosing God's Prosperity

One vivid childhood memory is when my father became ill. I do not remember what the illness was, but it happened suddenly. In time, he was physically fine. I remember he and my mother having a conversation at his hospital bed. He told her that one particular week he had held back giving his tithe to the church and he felt the Lord let the illness come upon him to teach him a lesson. That etched into my mind the importance of fearing God. He is very serious about our living according to His Word.

I have no idea whether God sent that brief physical setback into my father's life to teach him a lesson about giving. However, I am confident that God used the illness to get his attention and focus it again on spiritual priorities.

My father had a decision to make. It is the same decision millions of Christians make weekly. He could give the tithe to the Lord or use it to pay bills. Was he going to obey God or not? Dad chose not to tithe that week and he felt that God judged him for his disobedience. I do know that every week since that time he has chosen God's prosperity for his life.

Since the time that I began to make money, I have honored the Lord with at least one-tenth of everything I have earned. Most of the time I have never considered that I had an option regarding obedience or disobedience in this area. Therefore, I have never thought about what I could do with that money. I have known that God's blessing of prosperity would be on my life as I honored Him in giving.

The amount of salary or the number of bills has nothing to do with your giving. The issue is obedience to God.

Please do not misunderstand me. There were times while attending seminary, having children, and earning a modest salary that money has not been there. At the same time, we have always honored the Lord in giving, and we have never been late paying a bill. The amount of salary or the number of bills has nothing to do with your giving. The issue is obedience to God. When a person is obedient to God's Word and learns the importance of managing the money that God has given to him, the Lord's prosperity will come to his life.

The challenge I have is to grow each year in giving. Because I am a pastor, I have led out in giving in many building campaigns. This encouraged me to increase my giving annually. There have been years when we have given one-fourth of our income to the Lord's work. I do not share this information with you to boast, but so that you will know that I believe in what I am sharing with you on this subject.

I have discovered that it is difficult to teach, preach, talk about, or write about something that you do not experience personally. Giving is not taught, but caught. You must be willing to step out in obedience to God and choose His prosperity for your life.

Because we have been committed to the principle of tithing and giving through our local church, God has blessed us in extraordinary ways. Anyone who knows us well can tell you how God has stepped in on many occasions and blessed us in miraculous ways. They are gifts of grace which God bestows upon us because of simple obedience. The Bible says in Luke 16:10–11, "He who is faithful in a very little thing is faithful also in much; and he who is unrighteous in a very little thing is unrighteous also in much. If therefore you have not been faithful in the use of unrighteous mammon, who will entrust the true riches to you?"

As Jesus taught this principle to people, He wanted them to understand that when God could trust them with little things, He would be more inclined to trust them with bigger things in life. This principle is true not only in regard to money, but in every area of life.

As the sovereign God has stepped into our lives as an act of grace, He has also stepped into our lives in response to our faithfulness in the little things. As a result, our prayer is that we will be faithful to the Lord continually in our lives. Diligent service and obedience to Christ is a must, even in matters that may appear to be small or insignificant around you. Only then will your obedience and service warrant the Lord entrusting you with more in life, whatever that more may be.

Defining Prosperity

When money is the subject, Satan has a way to twist the truth to cause division and dissension. Years ago I made a commitment to teach only what the Word of God says about money.

What Prosperity Is Not

There is a heretical doctrine being taught today. It is known as prosperity gospel and can be summed up with the following phrase: If you give to the Lord, He will make you healthy, wealthy, and wise. This is a comfortable, upper middle-class heresy. Much of the world is desperately poor. The gospel of Jesus Christ works just as powerfully on a dusty African plain as it does in a carpeted urban church.

The prosperity that I find in God's Word does not teach that when you give money, God will bless you in an extravagant, material way. This false teaching is taught by those who have a poor understanding of God and His Word. Many have a selfish motivation in teaching this heresy because they are trying to increase the gifts to their ministry. God, in His sovereignty, may choose to extravagantly bless individuals in accordance with their giving. However, this is not a universal principle that needs to be taught, since it does not have merit from the Word of God.

One of my major struggles with this false teaching of prosperity gospel is that many who teach it believe that all money, if given to their particular ministry, will bring about this material extravagance. The first one-tenth of what God gives us is to go to our *local church,* excluding any other Christian organization. I believe firmly that this is the stance of Holy Scripture. Anything beyond the first tenth of what God gives us can be given to any Christian ministry which God has led us to support.

The kind of prosperity I am talking about does not teach that when you give, the Lord will make you healthy. This is rooted in the teaching that all sickness is from Satan. Scripture never supports this teaching. Some sickness is given directly from the Lord so that He may receive glory through it.

If I believed this heretical teaching, I would have had very serious questions in 1990 when my wife was diagnosed with cancer. Did this come from Satan? Absolutely not! Through her healing and ministry to others, God has received much glory. Did this mean that even though we were giving over twenty percent of our income to the Lord, we needed to give more? No! No credence can be given to this heretical view of prosperity not only biblically, but practically.

Prosperity gospel is not what I am referring to when I speak about prosperity from the Bible. The shame is that so much false teaching has been put forth on this subject that it is difficult to accept or appreciate any of the truth about it. Therefore, we need to clarify what prosperity is. Then, we need to choose prosperity daily in our lives.

What Prosperity Is

Prosperity is having your needs met plus some! Our basic needs in life can be understood from the sixth chapter of Matthew where Jesus said, "But seek first His kingdom and His righteousness; and all these things shall be added to you. Therefore do not be anxious for tomorrow; for tomorrow will care for itself. Each day has enough trouble of its own." When you seek first the kingdom of God and His righteousness, what are "these things" that will be added to you?

These things are the basic needs of life, such as what you will eat, drink, wear. Jesus said these things, when sought above the kingdom of God, will cause great anxiety. They will make you weary. Yet when you are willing to seek God and His kingdom above them, He will bless you with them in your life. What more do we really need other than these things?

Choosing prosperity will guarantee you that your needs will be met, and other things will be added that are simply blessings of grace.

This is why I define prosperity as having your needs met (food, drink and clothing) plus some. This "some" is anything other than what one eats, drinks, or wears. Therefore, we are very blessed by the Lord under this definition.

Choosing prosperity will guarantee you that your needs will be met, and other things will be added that are simply blessings of grace. These needs and these blessings of God's grace are guaranteed for you when you honor the Lord with at least one-tenth of everything that He has entrusted to you.

When you do not choose prosperity God's way and attempt to obtain it your way, you are opening yourself to the Lord's discipline. You are certainly going to experience much weariness and anxiety as well. None of this honors the Lord. Therefore, choose prosperity God's way—according to His Word!

Understanding Prosperity

If I were to offer you an insurance policy that would take care of your present needs as long as you live and all the future needs for your family after you die, would you be interested?

Without a doubt, you would be willing to listen to my sales pitch because of what the policy could do for you now and for your family in the future. Each of us is looking for something that will give us security. We are interested in anything that will guarantee us a blessed present and future.

To my knowledge, there is no policy available today that will care for every need in your life now and for every need your family will have after you die. If one did exist, the cost would be astronomical and those who could afford it would not need it.

Perhaps that's why our ears seem deafened when we are told that God wants to meet our needs, plus some. We've heard too many bizarre sales pitches. God Himself stands behind this offer. You can count on God. You have His Word on it.

What does the Bible teach about prosperity? Let's begin with the basics.

Understanding Stewardship

In order to understand stewardship from a biblical perspective, we must understand that it is grounded in the doctrine of God. Psalm 24:1–2 gives us a glimpse. "The earth is the Lord's, and all it contains, the world, and those who dwell in it. For He has founded it upon the seas, and established it upon the rivers."

The doctrine of God is best understood when we understand that everything on this earth, including the earth itself, belongs to God. God created it and God owns it. We see this verified again in Psalm 50:10–12. "For every beast of the forest is Mine, the cattle on a thousand hills. I know every bird of the mountains, and everything that moves in the field is Mine. If I were hungry, I would not tell you; for the world is Mine, and all it contains."

God makes it clear through His Word that everything in this world belongs to Him. The doctrine of God consists of God owning all, being all, having all, and demanding our all in life.

Stewardship begins with our understanding that God owns everything. I own nothing. Regardless of how hard I work to obtain things, none of them belongs to me. One of the errors people make is thinking that God owns only the first tenth of what they have. Absolutely not! God owns everything. If you do not give at least one-tenth to the Lord's work through your local church, it is because you do not understand that you own nothing and God owns absolutely everything.

Understanding stewardship also involves understanding accountability. We are accountable to God for what we have done with what He has entrusted to us. One day we will give an account of our lives to God. In this account, we will have to answer to Him for our relationship to the various things He has given to us.

Even though we own nothing, God has placed us as temporary keepers or managers of His possessions. In Genesis 1:26 the Bible says, "Then God said, 'Let Us make man in Our image, according to Our likeness; and let them rule over the fish of the sea and over the birds of the sky and over the cattle and over all the earth, and over every creeping thing that creeps on the earth.'"

The Old Testament word for stewardship is found in the word, *rule.* In the Hebrew language it is the word *radah,* meaning "I rule," limited to human dominion alone. This means we are given the authority by God to rule over the rest of God's creation.

In the New Testament, we learn the doctrine of stewardship from Jesus. It is found in Luke 16:2. "Give an account of your stewardship, for you can no longer be steward." Jesus' reference to stewardship in this passage comes from the Greek word, *oikonomos*. This word means to be a manager of an estate or an inspector of goods. Our God-given role is to manage the estate, the things that have been entrusted to us by the Lord. Remember, they all belong to Him, but He asks us to manage them for Him. We are accountable to the owner, Jesus Christ, for the way they are managed.

If we are going to choose prosperity in our lives, we need to understand biblical stewardship. Prosperity must be viewed against the backdrop of stewardship. It is impossible to keep prosperity biblically based if we are in error about the subject of stewardship.

Understanding Giving

Do you believe that God gives to us in proportion to how we give to Him? The Bible says in 2 Corinthians 9:6–9,

> Now this I say, he who sows sparingly, shall also reap sparingly; and he who sows bountifully shall also reap bountifully. Let each one do just as he has purposed in his heart; not grudgingly or under compulsion; for God loves a cheerful giver. And God is able to make all grace abound to you, that always having all sufficiency in everything, you may have an abundance for every good deed.

I believe this Scripture teaches us that the Lord gives to us in proportion to our giving to Him. If we give sparingly, we will reap sparingly. If we give to the Lord bountifully, we will reap bountifully. This principle is true for all areas of life, not just in giving money.

As we give, the passage above encourages us to give in a cheerful manner. The word *cheerful* means to be hilarious. I must admit that I know few hilarious givers, but this attitude is essential if we are to receive grace from the Lord in our giving. Ask God to make you a cheerful giver.

Understanding giving means we need to understand sacrifice. In the New Testament church we read of a few occasions when people gave everything they had to the Lord and His work. Acts 4:31–37 tells the story of the early Christians in Jerusalem. They were able to give everything away because they understood that they owned nothing.

> *Prosperity is never selfish...never resentful... It never hoards what it has.*

As we understand what God teaches about giving, we realize that we need to become unselfish, cheerful, and sacrificial in our giving. If we are to choose prosperity, we need to be continually reminded of these attitudes. Prosperity is never selfish, but unselfish. It is never resentful, but cheerful. It never hoards what it has, but it is willing to sacrifice it to the glory of God. These attitudes help us understand prosperity from a biblical perspective.

Understanding Missions

Why are we here? What is the purpose of the church? We discover answers to these questions in Matthew 28:19–20. "Go therefore and make disciples of all nations, baptizing them in the name of the Father and the Son and the Holy Spirit, teaching them to observe all that I commanded you; and lo, I am with you always, even to the end of the age."

We are here to make disciples all over the world. We are here to win people to Christ, baptize them, and teach them how to be obedient to the Lord. This commission of Jesus is to be the passion of our lives.

This passion of our lives needs to be kept in mind continually as we relate to the possessions that God has entrusted to us. The Bible says in Matthew 6:19, "Do not lay up for yourselves treasures upon the earth." These treasures are the things that we value in life. Jesus is encouraging us not to treasure the things of this earth. This earth is passing away.

When you synthesize these two biblical concepts, a dynamic spiritual principle emerges. We should make available all the resources that God has entrusted to us in order to further His Kingdom. Our calling is to share Jesus with the world. When I understand why I am here, then I must make all of the resources that God has given me available to Him for His use to take His message across the world. This is understanding missions, and it enables me to keep a balanced view of prosperity as I choose it for my life.

Understanding the Holy Spirit

Volumes have been written about the Holy Spirit. I want to highlight one verse of Scripture that teaches one of the roles of the Holy Spirit in our lives. The Bible says in John 16:13, "But when He, the Spirit of truth, comes, He will guide you into all the truth." One of the roles of the Holy Spirit is to teach us truth and to guide us into truth.

Understanding the Holy Spirit is essential in choosing prosperity because only He can build accurate views about stewardship, giving, and missions in your life. He is the only One Who can keep you balanced in your understanding of prosperity. The Holy Spirit is the only one who can build an unselfish, cheerful, and sacrificial attitude.

Understanding stewardship, giving, missions, and the Holy Spirit are essential to understanding prosperity. Prosperity is having your needs met, plus some. Choosing prosperity for your life is understanding that God owns everything and you own nothing. God has given you the privilege of managing His possessions. Choosing prosperity needs to be kept in balance by demonstrating attitudes that are unselfish, cheerful, and sacrificial. Choosing prosperity reminds me that I am here to take the gospel to the world; therefore, I need to be willing to make all of God's resources available to Him for His use in this endeavor.

Choosing prosperity for my life also calls me to be sensitive to the Holy Spirit. I need Him to keep me in balance and to create within me a proper biblical view of prosperity. As I embrace these essentials to understanding prosperity, I am now ready to experience it personally.

How to Experience Prosperity

Biblical prosperity is a choice which leads to real success. What actions do we need to take in order to experience prosperity?

Trust in the Lord

The first step is to trust in the Lord. The Bible says in Proverbs 28:25, "An arrogant man stirs up strife, but he who trusts in the Lord will prosper." An arrogant man trusts in himself. A prosperous man trusts in the Lord.

Are you trusting in the Lord or in yourself? In order to place your trust in the Lord, you must abandon self and cast yourself upon the mercy of God. Through this action, you will learn to trust in the Lord. A choice to trust in the Lord every day of my life is a choice to experience prosperity.

Live Right

The second step is to live in a right manner. A person who trusts in the Lord will live in a right manner. If you live rightly before the Lord, you will experience prosperity.

The Bible records what happens in our lives when we live righteously before the Lord. It says in Proverbs 11:28, "He who trusts in his riches will fall, but the righteous will flourish like the green leaf."

A righteous person does not trust in his riches, but in the Lord. This will make the righteous person flourish or experience prosperity. The Bible also says in Proverbs 28:13, "He who conceals his transgressions will not prosper, but he who confesses and forsakes them will find compassion."

A righteous person will not hide his sins, but will confess them and leave them behind him. The result for the righteous person—prosperity.

Live right before the Lord and before the world. It is a choice that enables you to experience prosperity. It is a choice that guarantees you real success.

Honor God from Your Wealth

Whatever you have in life is wealth because you own nothing. God owns it all. The Bible says in Proverbs 3:9–10, "Honor the Lord from your wealth, and from the first of all your produce; so your barns will be filled with plenty, and your vats will overflow with new wine."

> *The only tangible way that God has given for us to love Him is to honor Him with at least the first tenth of all He has entrusted to us.*

This is a great instruction. God calls us to place value on Him by giving Him at least one-tenth of all He has given us. This shows that we love Him, fear Him, and respect Him and our Lord. The only *tangible* way that God has given for us to love Him is to honor Him with at least the first tenth of all He has entrusted to us.

As we honor Him this way in our lives, we are promised a life of plenty and prosperity. Our needs will be met by the Lord, plus some. This is prosperity guaranteed. It is guaranteed not by a slick salesman or insurance policy, but by God Himself. You cannot beat such a guarantee.

Do you want to experience prosperity? God has promised it to you if you will honor Him with at least one-tenth of all He has entrusted to you. This will relieve you of the stress and worries of life. Your trust will be solely in the Lord and His Word. As you honor Him, He has promised you blessings in your life.

Do you want real success in your life? The kind of success that lasts forever? Of the many options you have before you, you must choose the right ones if you are going to experience success. One of these choices is prosperity—not some false, vain, selfish, and unbiblical view of prosperity but God's view of prosperity as described in His Word.

Be faithful to honor God with at least one-tenth of all He has entrusted to you through your local church. When this type of honor is given to the Lord, He has personally promised that He will step into your life and grant you prosperity—the kind of prosperity that will meet all your needs, plus some. What a guarantee! Choose prosperity today.

❧

T E N

Choosing Accountability

One of the greatest movements in Christianity today is the accountability movement. Accountability groups consisting of three to seven people are rising up across the country. Thousands of people are attending these groups weekly. Their main purpose is to hold one another accountable concerning spiritual, family, and ethical practices.

For years we have seen our nation reap the harvest of people who were not accountable. Promises are broken in marriage and family, in business and in government. Broken promises and compromised integrity have resulted in a fragmented, untrusting, and dysfunctional society.

In response to these problems, Bill McCartney, head football coach at Colorado University, founded a ministry called *Promise Keepers*. In the summer of 1993, Promise Keepers drew over fifty thousand men to Boulder, Colorado. Why has there been such a ground swell of support for being accountable and for encouraging others to keep promises in their lives? It is remarkable to see this happening across America, mainly because much of the movement is among the men of our country. Years ago, if anyone had said this would be happening today, few would have believed it. However, God is creating this desire for a return to accountability and a zeal to keep promises which we make to Him and to others.

> God is creating this desire for a return to accountability and a zeal to keep promises which we make to Him and to others.

The integrity crisis has crept into the lives of political leaders. We have seen on national television some of these leaders defending their integrity in a most ineffective manner, all because they could not continually cover up the truth. Many of our children's heroes are part of this group in which integrity is a thing of the past. These so called "role models" have now lost their influence on the children of our nation because of their questionable integrity. Some of our nation's religious leaders have embarrassed Christianity by their lack of integrity in the business operations of their ministry. What a tragedy it has been to see major newspapers and television specials spotlighting these who have lost their integrity.

Another reason this accountability movement has grown so rapidly is because of the excessive moral failure in our nation. This moral failure has taken place through the terrible sin of adultery. Whenever one is not mentally, emotionally, and sexually faithful to their spouse, they are committing adultery. Adultery is a sin. It is the worst kind of moral failure. It will result in a lack of trust, broken hearts, and many times, broken relationships that will never be repaired.

Moral failure has become a major problem in the church. It has become accepted by many. The rationalization and irresponsibility which is taking place is a disgrace to the church of Jesus Christ when the moral failure is permitted and simply receives a wink rather than a rebuke. Some churches are once again placing an emphasis on church discipline which calls Christians to be accountable, especially in the area of their moral responsibility to their families and the family of God. I believe that the great disappointments we have all experienced by the moral failure of some of the leaders of Christianity has done as much as anything to spark this movement of accountability. The attitude has been, "If it has happened to some of our greatest leaders, it could happen to me." Therefore, accountability has resurfaced in Christianity.

Situational ethics is another reason accountability has risen to a new level in Christianity. Compromising situations are threatening many people in the business world. Others are struggling with moral choices that are accepted by the world but are not permissible in the Word of God. Extreme stress that leads to a lifestyle full of work and no play has contributed to the rationalism that leads to an acceptance of situational ethics. The bottom line is that our ethical practices should never be determined by our situations in life but by the Word of God. What God says, He means. Therefore, we must obey Him regardless of the consequences we may face.

Accountability has been raised to a new level because of the integrity crisis, moral failure, and the acceptance of situational ethics in our society. People want to live in safety from a society being destroyed by lack of moral fiber, integrity, and ethics.

If we desire real success in life, it will only come if we make the right choices. These are choices toward God.

One of the choices toward God is to live in the safety of a relationship with the Lord. Choosing safety means you cannot live your life alone, but in accountability to others and to God. Sometimes this is painful. At other times it may be one of your greatest struggles. However, in the end, living your life being accountable to others is one of the greatest choices you will ever make. Why? Because it is a choice to real success. Success that is not temporary, but eternal. The kind of success that will help you finish the race of life in an admirable and godly fashion.

The Negatives of a Solitary Life

When a person does not choose to live in accountability to others, he chooses a solitary life. A solitary person has few, if any, friends and lives a lonely life. The solitary life is addressed in Ecclesiastes 4:9–10, "Two are better than one because they have a good return for their labor. For if either of them falls, the one will lift up his companion. But woe to the one who falls when there is not another to lift him up."

The Bible discourages living a solitary life by pointing out that it can be dangerous. If you fall, who will be there to pick you up? Since the Scripture does not encourage it, what are some of the negatives of a solitary life?

Open to Sin

Whenever you choose a solitary life, you are opening your life to sin. When there is no one in your life asking the hard questions, you will be bent toward sin. When you are not hearing truth expounded from the Word of God, you are opening your life to sin. When you are lacking in meaningful relationships there will be little accountability in your life.

When you are lacking in meaningful relationships there will be little accountability in your life.

The writer of Ecclesiastes gives brilliant advice. Judgment will result in the life of a person who lives without the help of others. You can fall into a sin some might consider minor. But before you know it, you will sink into the pit of what is considered major sin. Some sins could be avoided through having someone in your life serving as your spiritual encourager.

What we do in private really shows our level of spirituality. Do we pray and honor God in private? Do we fill ourselves with materials and experiences which diminish our walk with Christ? In private times and places, our choices can be threatening. These private places in a solitary life can easily serve as areas in which we fall into sin. A solitary life is vulnerable to sin.

Vulnerable to Depression

There are times when being alone is healthy for each of us. Jesus spent much time alone, but He was never lonely. Loneliness is one of the leading emotional problems in America today. Loneliness leads to depression. Depression is the feeling of being downcast, discouraged, and dismayed.

Whenever you choose a solitary life you are vulnerable to depression. Paradoxically, it is when you are depressed that you do not want to be around others. Yet being around others is the very thing that will help you through your depression. Safety is exchanged for danger when one lives a solitary life.

Elijah had just experienced great victory with God. Ahab and Jezebel had killed many of God's prophets and were in hot pursuit of Elijah for the same purpose. Elijah succeeded in escaping to a cave. From this cave he cried to God in self-pity, saying he was the only one who was serving Him. He was depressed.

The "Elijah syndrome" is experienced by many of us. When you become depressed your perspective is blurred. You lose focus and eventually lose spiritual power. If you have isolated yourself from others for a period of time there may not be anyone there to pick you up when you are depressed. This is definitely a danger in living your life apart from others.

Uncontrollable Ego

Whenever a person lives apart from others, his ego can get out of control. Meaningful relationships are effective in taming our egos. This is important because an uncontrollable ego can produce many problems.

It can produce extreme selfishness, the kind of selfishness that never considers what is best for others, the team, a business, church, or family. An uncontrollable ego can also produce a temperament that is quick to wrath and judgment. This causes many problems in a person's life when they have isolated themselves and then are placed in a situation in which they are dependent on others for the success of their performance. An uncontrollable ego leads to insensitivity to other people, their feelings, and their opinions. If I am insensitive to others, it is usually because my ego is out of control, deceiving me into believing I am more important than others.

The truth is that no person is an island to themselves. There is not one of us who can have a healthy existence totally away from others. Therefore, an attempt to live a solitary life has many negative implications, not only for us personally, but for those with whom we must relate in some way.

Therefore, we must refuse to live a solitary life. It is not wise, biblical, or fair to anyone. Life is bigger than all of us. We may be dispensable in our jobs, but we are indispensable in the sense that we are created by God to contribute uniquely to life with the gifts, talents, and abilities He has given us. So choose more for yourself. Choose accountability by relating to others in a godly way.

The Value of Others

Since living an isolated life is not beneficial, we need another strategy, one that recognizes others have tremendous value to your life. Think through this subject with me as we consider our relationship to others.

The Value of Counselors

When I say counselors, I am not referring to the professionals who operate in the field. I am referring to people who are close to you that give you counsel about your life. This could be a professional counselor, but for most people this would not be the case. Professional Christian counselors have their place in the body of Christ. As a pastor, I am always willing to refer people to a professional Christian counselor if their need demands it. I realize that my gifts are limited in this area and that others can help people in ways I cannot. Remember, I am talking here only about the people who give you counsel to you about your life.

Each of us faces situations when we need counsel from others. If a person chooses to live independently, not seeking the counsel of others, he or she is foolish. This lack of wisdom can have negative implications, some of which have been mentioned already.

Who are the people who give you counsel? It is important to get counsel from people who view life from God's perspective. This is the only way godly counsel will be given to you. Just having a group of people give their advice is not enough. They need to be godly people who understand life from His perspective and who will be able to relate principles for spiritual living.

Are these counselors valuable? The Bible says they are. In Proverbs 11:14 we read, "Where there is no guidance, the people fall, but in abundance of counselors there is victory."

The counselors who provide wise, godly counsel keep us from falling into sin, and give us guidance and direction for living. When we seek their godly counsel and consider it strongly in our decision-making process, there will be victory. In other words, God's will is able to be done.

How many counselors should one have to receive godly counsel? I believe it is important to have no less than three people, but not more than five. The reason for this is that too few people will give you a limited perspective about your problem or decision. Too many people giving you counsel could bring confusion and endanger the confidentiality of your situation.

These people should come from various backgrounds in life. They do not need to be the same type of people with similar spiritual gifts and temperaments. This will limit the diversity of views you will receive from them. When the term "abundance of counselors" is used, I do not believe it means masses of people, but various people from different walks in life. Victory is promised in an abundance of counselors.

Such counselors for your life may be able to help you reach some of the goals and dreams you have. The Bible says in Proverbs 15:22, "Without consultation, plans are frustrated, but with many counselors they succeed."

So many times we make plans for our lives. These plans are often placed on the shelf. If we had been willing to risk telling others about our plans, they could have given us some consultation on how the plans could be realized. Frustration is a result of not sharing your dreams, goals, and desires with others.

As a pastor, I have learned that if I am willing to risk telling others some things that are stirring in my heart, God is able to bring many of these things into my life and ministry. We cannot fear rejection if we are going to seek counsel from others. They serve as our protection. In my life, they do not exist to tell me what I want to hear, but what I need to hear. If they genuinely love God and me, then they are seeking to make me successful in my life and ministry.

We cannot fear rejection if we are going to seek counsel from others. They serve as our protection.

I remember gathering a group of men together to help plan the future of our church. After we had done much planning as a pastoral team, we took our thoughts and plans to this group. In time, I felt that though the vast majority of them felt it was a good plan, they were just not convinced it was God's plan. I let time take its course. We went back to the drawing board. After many months, we connected with God's plan and we received unbelievable support. In the meantime, God had cleared obstacles for us enabling the new plan to gain support.

Years ago, I would have spiritualized the experience and gone ahead and done what I wanted to do. Through the years, I have learned that I am not always right. I do not always have God's mind in every situation. Therefore, I need to lean on others to assist me in determining the will of God.

Counselors will help bring about your success. They will help you realize your plans and fulfill your goals. A wise person will seek counsel from others.

Sometimes life seems to be a war. The reason it seems that way is that it is. Spiritual discernment would remind me that my battle is not with people, but with the forces of Satan. He is trying to destroy my life. What do I need in the war of life as I face these battles? The Bible says in Proverbs 24:6, "For by wise guidance you will wage war, and in abundance of counselors there is victory."

We need wise guidance as we face the battles of our lives. This wise guidance will only come from the counselors in our lives who are living out their faith according to the Word of God. Guidance alone is not enough. It needs to be wise guidance.

Once again in the Scripture we are promised victory as we seek the counsel of godly, wise people in our lives. It takes spiritual maturity to permit others to dream your dreams with you and help you reach your goals in life. As you mature in the Lord, wise guidance is respected and appreciated rather than ignored.

Others do have great value to me in my spiritual life. They can help me realize many dreams in my life. They can help me live in spiritual victory rather than spiritual defeat. Thank God for the other people in your life, especially those who serve as your wise counsel.

The Value of a Listening Ear

Years ago a great man of God fell into moral sin. It was the leading story on every major television affiliate in his metropolitan area. The front page story the next morning in all the papers was about the moral fall of this pastor. It was a sad experience that I will never forget because this man had a major, positive effect on my ministry.

As his sin was evaluated by many people, the question in their minds was, "Was he a part of a group that made him accountable for his life?" The surprising answer was the he did participate enthusiastically in such a group every week. Obviously he successfully deceived them. A few of those men had attempted to give him good counsel, but he did not choose to listen. Counsel is worthless if you are not willing to listen to it.

This does not mean that you should always do what you are counseled because God may want you to do something that requires simple trust of Him alone. However, in regard to integrity, morality, and ethical practices, you must listen to the counselors in your life. They may be able to recognize the many blind spots you cannot see.

Listening is a critically important skill to develop in our lives. The Bible says in Proverbs 25:11-12, "Like apples of gold in settings of silver is a word spoken in right circumstances. Like an earring of gold and an ornament of fine gold Is a reprover to a listening ear."

By using these similes, the writer is helping us understand the value of good listening. A graceful word, spoken at the right time in a certain circumstance, is like golden apples in a silver setting. They stand out to everyone who hears them. Someone who is willing to be honest with you about your life can be as precious as a golden earring or ornament if you will listen to them. Having people who are honest with you is no guarantee of your success, however; real success comes only when you choose to develop a listening ear.

We need to choose to be teachable, willing learners throughout our lives. A person who will not listen to others is not such a person. They are not willing to submit themselves to others. Ephesians 5:21 reminds us to "be subject to one another in the fear of Christ."

We always need to be willing to place ourselves under another out of our love and respect for Jesus Christ. If I do not fear God, I will not listen to others. If I fear God, then I will listen to others.

I realize that God may be using people to speak to my life about the decisions or issues that are relevant at the time.

Are you teachable? Do you place yourself under the authority of others? Are you willing to listen to the people who surround your life? Pray for God to give you a humble heart and a willingness to listen to others. Ask the Lord to help you see the big picture of how He may be using these people to speak to you.

Sometimes through wise counsel God may share the burdens of others with you. Galations 6:2 says, "Bear one another's burdens, and thus fulfill the law of Christ." The law of Jesus Christ is to love the Lord and to love others. Love calls you to have a listening ear when others seek your counsel, not simply for your own personal gain, but to help them bear the burdens of their lives.

Love calls you to have a listening ear when others seek your counsel.

There is much value in developing a listening ear. The rewards are great. The blessings are many. Choose to listen to wise, godly counsel around you and to be such a listener to others. It is a choice to real success.

The Value of Discipline

As we learn to listen to wise counsel, sometimes the honesty of it may force us to deal with difficult issues in our lives. We do not need people around us who will tell us what we want to hear, but we need people who will tell us what we need to hear. The Bible says, "Listen to counsel and accept discipline, that you may be wise the rest of your days"(Prov. 19:20).

Will you accept discipline if your group of wise, godly counselors thinks you need it? If they discipline you—meaning correct you when your missteps start you down the wrong path of your life—will you be willing to change directions?

When you are wise enough to accept the discipline of those around us, your days will be filled with wisdom. You will be able to see life the way God sees it and make the right choices in your life. One of these right choices is to listen and accept discipline when you need it.

Just as a boat on the ocean may deviate from its course due to the wind or weather, we do the same in life's storms and changing circumstances. Just as a boat has checkpoints to follow on its charted course, our checkpoints are brought to the surface by wise and godly people who want the best for us in life. Therefore, we need to receive their discipline, their correction to get us to our destination.

> *Choosing accountability is understanding that you need others to surround you in your life to give you wise and godly counsel.*

Sometimes it is a personal threat to have strong people around your life. On the church staff that serves with me there are all kinds of personalities. Some of these staff members are considered very strong people. Typically a leader is threatened when those around are stronger than he in certain areas, but I learned a long time ago to surround myself with winners. I have no need to fear strong people who are willing to be honest with me. The staff is under my leadership, but when major decisions are being made about the ministry of our church, they help me make them. They are not robots programmed to agree with me, but wise counselors about ministry. Iron does sharpen iron. Those strong, godly men will only help me to be better and push me to be better for God in my personal life and ministry.

Choosing accountability is understanding that you need others to surround you in your life to give you wise and godly counsel. Choosing accountability is a wise choice prompting real spiritual success.

I have always been intrigued with various types of trees. Years ago, I learned about the redwood trees in California. Just recently, I was reminded of one of the great things about these trees. Their root system is unlike most other trees with root systems that grow deep into the ground. The roots of redwood trees are not that way. In fact, the roots are small in comparison to the huge, towering trees.

Their unique root system results when the roots of several redwoods grow together and intertwine, giving them extraordinary strength so that they are able to withstand various weather conditions which otherwise could jeopardize their survival.

This is how believers are to live together. We grow more mature in Christ and grow together and become a mighty force. We need one another for strength and support. Then when the various storms in life blow our way, we can tower before the world as God's instruments, just as the redwood trees tower in the skies through their adversities.

Choose accountability. Intertwine your life with others. You will be stronger. You will be better for God. You will survive the storms of life. You will experience genuine success—God's power!

❧

ELEVEN

Choosing Spiritual Victory

One of the greatest fears in modern day America is the fear of failure. In the world of business, not reaching an expected monthly quota is considered failure. Chief executive officers are dropping like flies because of their perceived failure by their boards or stockholders. In the experience of parenting, which I believe is the toughest job in the world, parents are viewed as failures if one of their children falls by the wayside.

In life, many are failures because they lack the right look—a lean, tanned body wearing designer clothes. In the world of athletics, if the win and loss columns do not satisfy the athletic director, alumni, or now even some of the players, coaches with proven ability are put out on the street and viewed as failures.

Our society is success oriented. If you journey through a bookstore, you will quickly discover the emphasis placed on success just by scanning the titles of various books. Our success craze has jeopardized the meaning of real success.

There is also a tendency to equate worldly success with spiritual success. Beware of making this costly mistake.

The World's View of Success

Success in the eyes of the world is distorted compared to the success mentioned in the Word of God. I want to highlight some specific things that the world system would consider success.

The world views power as success. Power is having influence over others. Power is influencing the direction of an organization. Power means that you can do anything you want to do without any limits being placed on you. Power is viewed, at times, as having no accountability to others because of a great position or outstanding ability. The major problem with viewing power as success is that not everyone in the world can have power. Therefore, few people can be successful.

Popularity is viewed as success. Popularity is being well liked and having the approval of others. This is how so many people attempt to determine their self-worth. What a negative trap this is if one determines his personal worth based on his popularity. Since everyone cannot be popular, everyone cannot experience success as the world views it.

The world system propagates a belief that success is determined by the possessions you have. These possessions include money, material resources, or other things you have been able to accumulate. However, as we all know, not everyone can accumulate the same amount of possessions since not everyone has the resources to do so. This view is erroneous because so many people would be eliminated from the race for success if this was really its criterion.

The world system also tells us that success is determined by who you know and who knows you. It is so easy to get caught in this trap. Each of us has met people who like to drop names of powerful, rich, or popular people, implying they know them personally. These name-droppers have bought into the lie that success is determined by the people you know and who know you. The problem with this view of success is that not everyone has the opportunity to get to know a person of fame or influence.

You can never satisfy all your desires; therefore, could you ever be successful?

Sensual pleasure is also an ingredient in success according to the world. In pursuing sensual pleasure, society applauds sexual prowess and promiscuity of all kinds. This is why chastity is seen not only as frivolous and unimportant but silly.

Many who promote the world's view of success would have us also believe that recreation and enjoyment are needed to experience success. Our society has an insatiable hunger to enjoy life. Again, the acceptance of this view of success means it is unattainable. You can never satisfy all your desires; therefore, could you ever be successful?

The world system encourages greed in our lives. In fact, it is equated with success. The world will tell you that if you can just obtain this one thing more, whatever that thing may be, you will be satisfied. If this position is true, one can easily compromise ethics in order to be successful. Greedy people are never satiated. If success requires obtaining more and more, it is a vain view.

The world's view of success favors power, popularity, the accumulation of many possessions, knowing the right people, experiencing sensual pleasure, enjoying life through various recreational opportunities, and continually attempting to fulfill your desire for more in life. These interpretations of success are traps into which countless people have fallen.

Success so defined is limited and exclusive—limited in that it never views success from God's perspective and exclusive in that only the people able to achieve or acquire these things can be considered successful. Few people ever succeed in even one of these areas, much less all of them.

It is sad that so many people makechoices in their lives which require that they buy into this vain philosophy of success. These are poor choices, because they do not lead them to real success; after they have made these poor choices, thinking they are guaranteed success, they discover only a feeling of emptiness. How tragic this is for the person who longs with his whole being to be successful. He discovers that his search has been in vain.

Since the quest for success in the world is a neverending and empty search, what is the source of authentic success? Where is it obtained in life? Real success in life will never be found in the world. Corrie and Betsie ten Boom found real success within the confines of a German concentration camp. They had no personal possessions, no power and no influence. They lived with the total absence of luxury, and yet they were successful because genuine success is living in spiritual victory. We need to choose spiritual victory in life.

Who Gives Real Spiritual Victory?

The desire of each believer should be to live in real spiritual victory. Obviously, spiritual victory does not come from the world. If it did, it would be temporal and empty as we have already seen. Real spiritual victory is not temporal. It is not tentative. Real spiritual victory is demonstrative. It will be expressed in every area of our lives. However, where does spiritual victory come from?

Human Preparation

Does human preparation mean that we determine spiritual victory? Oh yes, we can choose actions in our lives to lead us to spiritual victory, actions like reading God's Word, praying, worshiping, giving, and witnessing. However, these things might be more appropriately called results of our spiritual victory rather than actions that lead to spiritual victory. We make a mistake if we ever assume that we alone determine our spiritual victory.

Spiritual victory does not come through human preparation. The Bible says in Proverbs 21:31, "The horse is prepared for the day of battle, but victory belongs to the Lord." The horse can be prepared for the day of battle. He can be fed, watered, and trained for battle. However, this preparation does not bring victory. Victory belongs to the Lord. This means that God is the only One who really secures our victories in life.

Trusting in yourself and in what you can do to secure spiritual victory is a futile act. "If you are slack in the day of distress, your strength is limited" (Prov. 24:10). Each of us will undergo some days of distress. We cannot always be strong and sharp; therefore, you can count on it, your strength will be limited. The result will not be spiritual victory, but defeat.

Self-reliance is not a step toward spiritual victory but a step away from it. Self-dependence is not a result of spiritual victory but a sign of spiritual defeat. Any dependence on self for spiritual victory is a foolish choice to make. The question comes again, "Who gives real spiritual victory?"

Victory belongs only to the Lord. As He looks at your heart and sees your desires, He alone determines the spiritual victory that you will experience in your life.

"But thanks be to God, who gives us the victory through our Lord Jesus Christ" (1 Cor. 15:57). Earlier in this text, the apostle Paul wrote that death and the grave will not gain victory over us. He tells us that death is swallowed up in victory. How is this? Through the death and resurrection of Jesus Christ, death is defeated. He is speaking of everlasting spiritual victory, victory that escalates through death, our greatest trial of life, to an eternal victory of life. Only the Lord Jesus Christ can give this victory!

Through the years, I have adopted a philosophy of real success. Anytime I share this statement with others, I refer to the words as being life changing. My personal philosophy is: Real success never depends on your circumstances, real success depends on one specific relationship.

When you embrace the world's view of success, you cannot experience success throughout life. You cannot control the circumstances that bring this temporal success. Therefore, genuine success never depends on your circumstances. Circumstances will always change in your life. In fact, changing circumstances will be one constant thing you can count on in your life.

Genuine success depends on one relationship, a personal relationship with Jesus Christ. Once this relationship is formed, it will never end. Choosing a relationship with Jesus Christ is choosing real spiritual success. With the Lord in my life, I am successful. Once He enters my life, He will never leave me; therefore, I can be successful even in death. Since my Lord overcame death, I will overcome death.

> *Real success comes only from the Lord because of the personal relationship I have chosen to have with Him.*

Do not believe that success depends on circumstances. Real success depends on a relationship with Jesus Christ. People can have power, popularity, and possessions, know the right people, experience sensual pleasure, enjoy the recreational opportunities of life, and attempt to satisfy their greed; but if they do not have a relationship with Jesus, they are not experiencing real success, spiritual or otherwise.

Real success does not come from the things of the world, nor from anything that I can accomplish in my life. Real success comes only from the Lord because of the personal relationship I have chosen to have with Him.

Since the Lord alone gives us real success, the win and loss columns do not matter. The kind of clothes we wear does not matter. How others view us does not matter. The things of this world and the views of the people of this world do not matter to me. All these are temporary and will lead to emptiness in life. The Lord's victory is real and lasting.

Now that we have evaluated how the world views success, I believe it would be helpful to clarify what the Lord considers real success and victory.

Real Spiritual Victory

Joshua became Israel's leader following the death of Moses. The Lord gave Joshua some instructions that would help make him a successful leader.

> Only be strong and very courageous, to be careful to do according to all the law which Moses My servant commanded you; do not turn from it to the right or to the left, so that you may have success wherever you go. This book of the law shall not depart from your mouth, but you shall meditate on it day and night, so that you may be careful to do according to all that is written in it; for then you will make your way prosperous, and then you will have success. Have I not commanded you? Be strong and courageous! Do not tremble or be dismayed, for the Lord your God is with you wherever you go. (Josh. 1:7–9)

I believe these words give us the meaning of real spiritual victory. The Lord instructed Joshua not to deviate from what He told him, and he would be successful. The Lord strongly encouraged him to be faithful to His Word, and he would be successful. The Lord also told him that success would occur because of His presence with Joshua. This kind of success is real spiritual victory. I want to use this text and others to share with you the components of real spiritual victory.

The Presence of God

The greatest promise given to Joshua was that the Lord was going to be with him. What greater success can one have than the presence of the Lord? Joshua was told to be very strong and courageous as a leader. Fear and dismay were not to be experienced by him because the Lord was going to be with him wherever he would go.

Psalm 23:4 gives us a great promise regarding His presence: "Even though I walk through the valley of the shadow of death, I fear no evil; for Thou art with me; Thy rod and Thy staff, they comfort me."

> *Real spiritual victory will not come apart from the presence of the Lord with us.*

The greatest challenge each of us will face is the challenge of death, but God promises that we do not even have to fear that because He will be present to comfort us as we are ushered into eternity.

Real spiritual victory will not come apart from the presence of the Lord with us. His presence is spiritual victory. Once Jesus Christ comes into our lives, His presence is with us always. Therefore, we already have spiritual victory.

The Protection of God

God's presence serves as our protection in life. Joshua was told by God that he did not need to fear and that he was not to become disheartened. He was also told that no man would be able to stand against him. The Lord would not fail him or forsake him. Joshua was promised the protection of God. This is real spiritual victory!

One of the great stories in the Bible is the story of Job. God protected Job with a hedge of protection described in Job 1:10: "Hast Thou not made a hedge about him and his house and all that he has, on every side? Thou hast blessed the work of his hands, and his possessions have increased in the Land." Because of this hedge, nothing could touch Job, unless the Lord permitted it or removed the hedge from around him. That hedge was never removed from Job personally. Throughout his trials, the Lord preserved and restored him.

God is faithful to give you His protection. He has a vested interest in you and me. Nothing can touch our lives unless He permits it. Trusting in His protection and believing that this is true is real spiritual victory.

The Provision of God

As Joshua and the people of God entered the Promised Land, they experienced God's provision for their lives. As we give our lives to kingdom business, we are promised the provision of God for our personal needs. The Bible says in Philippians 4:19, "And my God shall supply all your needs according to His riches in glory in Christ Jesus."

His riches in glory are great because these riches are found in Jesus Christ. He is the ultimate provision for all of us. The provision of God is real spiritual victory. His provision is great! His provision is sufficient! His provision is everything!

The Prosperity of God

The Lord told Joshua that He would make him prosperous as he followed His Word. Remember, this prosperity meant having his needs met, plus some. This prosperity promised to Joshua was his spiritual success and victory.

The Lord promises His people prosperity as they follow His Word. In Ephesians 3:20 we read, "Now to Him who is able to do exceeding abundantly beyond all that we ask or think, according to the power that works within us." This means that God is able to do more for us than we can imagine to ask Him because of His mighty power that works within us. The prosperity of God is spiritual victory and one of the great blessings of life.

The Power of God

The Lord told Joshua that God's power would enable Him to take the promised land for the people of God. This power would go with him as long as he obeyed the Word the Lord gave to him as the leader of His people.

God's power is great. He can do more in a moment than we could ever do in a lifetime! The resurrected Christ told His disciples, "You shall receive power" (Acts 1:8). This is the power of the Holy Spirit given to empower us to share the gospel of Jesus Christ with the world. This power grows as our willingness to share the gospel increases.

God's power is the Holy Spirit living within us, the same power that raised Jesus from the dead. It is mountain-moving power as we exhibit faith in the Lord. Spiritual victory is God's power alive in His children.

The Possibilities for God

Joshua would be able to seize many opportunities for the Lord. They would come his way because of his deep dedication and devotion to the Lord. These possibilities would require him to have the power to make right choices for the Lord.

When we experience spiritual victory, we will be faced with many possibilities for the Lord. This is why Paul told us, "I can do all things through Him who strengthens me" (Phil. 4:13). The Lord will enable us through His strength to seize these opportunities. He is able to give us a "can-do" spirit to help us use every possibility for the glory of God.

> *Spiritual victory is seizing the opportunities and possibilities that God brings our way.*

Spiritual victory is seizing the opportunities and possibilities that God brings our way. We cannot ignore them or refuse any of them. They are God's possibilities for life. These possibilities provide us with spiritual victory.

The Person of God

Real success is knowing the Lord Jesus Christ. He is the person of God. Knowing Christ is knowing God. There is no spiritual victory apart from the Lord. He is your spiritual victory. Receiving spiritual victory is receiving Jesus Christ into your life.

Spiritual victory is the presence of God, the protection of God, the provision of God, the prosperity of God, the power of God, seizing the possibilities for God, and knowing the person of God, Jesus Christ. When you choose spiritual victory in your life, you will experience these wonderful components of spiritual victory.

These components all result from your relationship with Jesus Christ. They are dependable and consistent, much different than the success the world promotes through having the right circumstances. As appealing as they may be, circumstances cannot give you real spiritual victory because they are ever-changing. Our relationship with Jesus Christ never changes. Once we enter into a relationship with Him, we begin to experience the thrill of spiritual victory.

The world says that success is power, but God says it is His presence with us in life. The world believes that success is being popular, but God says it is His protection for our lives. The world is confident that success is the accumulation of possessions, but the Lord says that success is trusting Him to meet our needs, not following our selfish desires. The world tells us that success is knowing the right people in life, while the Lord says that success is experiencing the mighty power of God in our lives. The world propagates the belief that success is enjoying life through various forms of recreation, but God says success is seizing the various opportunities and possibilities that come our way as we follow Him. The world says that success is fulfilling our greedy desires, but God says it is knowing Him in a personal way.

Let me urge you to choose real success in your life. Do not settle for the world's view of success. It is temporary and empty. Choosing real success is something that will last for eternity. It is a choice that will lead to the power of God in your life. Choose real spiritual success in your life today.

❧

PART FOUR

Choices to Meaningful Relationships

CHOOSING MEANINGFUL RELATIONSHIPS

CHOOSING GOD'S BEST FOR YOUR CHILD

CHOOSING WHAT IS RIGHT
FOR THE NEXT GENERATION

CHOOSING JESUS

T W E L V E

Choosing Meaningful Relationships

Meaningful relationships are usually born through the experience of change. My university days provided the opportunity for many such relationships. It was in this setting that I met the woman who would become my wife. It was also in these university days that many friends were made who will be friends for life.

I had never visited the campus of Howard Payne University before I started to school there. I knew the school was located in a town of just over twenty thousand people in central Texas. I knew it was a Baptist university which trained young people for the ministry. When I arrived there in 1974, it seemed to be a pretty big place compared to where I had lived all my life.

I met Bruce and Pam at Howard Payne. Bruce Perkins from Frederick, Oklahoma, became valedictorian of our class. Pam

Ulmer was a city girl from Fort Worth, Texas. In a matter of time, Bruce and Pam met, and in God's timing, they fell in love. They married in January of 1977, just days after Jeana and I were married on December 31, 1976.

We lived two houses from each other just off the campus. Jeana and I lived in a cute duplex apartment that was extremely cold in the winter and very hot in the summer. Bruce and Pam lived in an old house. The main thing I remember about it was how cold it was on a night when we were there for a social event.

Within a year or year and a half, we all ended up in Fort Worth, Texas, attending Southwestern Baptist Theological Seminary. Our relationship continued to grow. We lived in homes just off the seminary campus, a few streets from one another.

In a matter of months, Bruce became a staff member at a church in the Fort Worth area and eventually became the pastor of this church. Then Jeana and I left the immediate area of Fort Worth when I became a full-time pastor in a church sixty miles from the seminary. In these separate settings, God began to build our ministries and continued to build our friendship.

In 1980, within a couple of months, each of us became parents to boys. Jeana and I were blessed with Josh, and Bruce and Pam with Matt. Then I entered the doctoral program making it necessary for me to stay in Fort Worth for days at a time. I lived with Bruce, Pam, and Matt in their church parsonage. Our friendship continued to deepen.

In 1981, the Lord called us to the Gulf Coast of Texas to pastor a church. We never let the relationship fall by the wayside although hundreds of miles separated us. In 1983, again just days apart, the Lord gave each of us another child, a little girl named Kalyn for the Perkins and our second son, Nicholas.

We have attended conventions together. We have vacationed together in Colorado and Texas. Every time Jeana and I go to the Dallas/Fort Worth area, we do our best to see Bruce and Pam. Our two families have chosen to have a meaningful relationship.

Several factors have contributed to the success of our relationship. The Perkins and the Floyds initially came together around the cross of Jesus Christ. It was a deep conviction of the need for a Christian education that brought us together at Howard Payne University.

Although we came from four different places, God brought us together in a special Christian relationship with each other. This is why our relationship has been meaningful. Whether it is in the hot summer visiting an amusement park called Fiesta Texas or tolerating Bruce's slow driving, our relationship has withstood many tests. We have survived all these challenges because it has been a Christian relationship.

I believe having the ministry in common is another reason we have enjoyed a meaningful relationship. Our love for the ministry and our desire for God to use us to the maximum has been a major common denominators in our relationship.

Without a doubt, our children are a blessing to each of us. Their children are ours and our children are theirs. We have attended Dallas Cowboy games, Texas Ranger games, Cotton Bowl games, and amusement parks together, mostly because of our children.

Jeana and Bruce have very similar personalities, and Pam and I are often told that we are alike in personality. Jeana and Bruce are always laid back, not really caring what decision is made. Pam and I are intense and care deeply about every decision; therefore, if conflict occurs, it is usually between Pam and me. The humorous thing is that Pam and I dated a few times in college and all agree that had she and I married, we possibly would have killed one another.

The Perkins and the Floyds have a meaningful relationship. We have made memories together. Hopefully, we will make many more, with few of them being in amusement parks. Our relationship is solid, one of highest integrity and love.

This relationship exists because we have made a choice to have a meaningful relationship. I do not think that we determined one day this would occur; it just happened. It happened because of Christ, the ministry, our children, and the many things we share in common.

One of the choices to God's power is to choose to experience meaningful relationships in life.

One of the choices to God's power is to choose to experience meaningful relationships in life. These relationships can be with friends or family, but the most important thing is that they are built on Jesus Christ. Meaningful relationships don't just happen. These relationships go through a process of growth and development. This process is a challenge, but also a joy as you go through it together.

Various Levels of a Relationship

Various levels exist in all relationships. It is quite naive to think that every relationship in your life is and should be on the same level. As you learn that there are various levels in a relationship, you will be ready to enter some meaningful relationships. Everyone cannot be your best friend and you cannot be a best friend to everyone. Therefore, I want you to think about the various levels that are involved in all the relationships in your life. I believe there are four levels which exist in all of them.

Level Four: Surface Relationships

Surface relationships are the most common of all relationships. These relationships are the foundationof all relationships. Every relationship begins as a surface relationship.

This level begins with an introduction, you begin by learning the other person's name and engaging in light, casual conversation. The surface relationship is tentative. There is no strong commitment from either person. In fact, there can be almost a passive approach to the relationship.

One common surface relationship not expected to progress to another level is with someone who waits on you in a store. The conversation rarely goes beyond how you are doing and talk about the weather. But all relationships begin at this level.

Level Three: Structured Relationships

When a relationship is ready to go to another level, it is usually because it has been structured to do so. Structured relationships are those that take place at a specific time each week. This may center around a recurring event in the same location. These structured relationships are built on routine encounters which reveal commonalities existing between people.

For example, when our children began playing sports, we began to meet new people at their games. Initially, these relationships were tentative and passive. However, as we encountered the same people week after week in a casual atmosphere, these relationships moved to another level. We were together at least twice a week at a baseball game in the park with children playing on the same baseball team. Structured relationships can occur in any number of ways, but usually happen around a common interest or activity in which you are involved.

Level Two: Secure Relationships

When a structured relationship becomes healthy and enjoyable, the relationship then moves to a new level which I call a secure relationship. The two parties desire to spend more time together. Mutual sharing begins to take place in all kinds of ways. At this level of a relationship, trust begins to form and becomes important as it grows. At this level, friendship can sometimes be tested. The most common test will usually involve trust.

Friendship can grow into personal friendship in a secure relationship. As you enjoy being with this person, you find you are comfortable with them in almost any situation. At this level, you begin to learn how much you can trust this person. This trust results in security as you feel good being together in most circumstances in which you find yourselves.

Level One: Solid Relationships

The goal of a relationship, once those involved are secure, should be for them to experience a solid relationship. This is the apex of all relationships. At this level, a long-term relationship is going to develop between you and the other person. In a solid relationship, complete trust and confidentiality exist. They are inseparable twins. Genuine love is expressed in the relationship without expecting anything in return. Even if time does not permit togetherness in the relationship, the relationship remains solid and deep through all the interims.

I believe these various levels of relationships are determined by the agreement that exists between the persons involved. People are not usually attracted to others in their lives where commonality and agreement do not exist. Life is filled with stress; therefore, meaningful relationships occur because of the things you have in common and agreements that take place.

An Interesting Observation

All relationships will be tested. In fact, the level of a relationship usually moves through a period of transition when a test occurs. The interesting observation I have made personally and pastorally about relationships is that the level of the relationship will be determined by the way those involved respond to the conflict. When a conflict is not dealt with properly, the relationship can regress to a previous level. When a conflict occurs and the response is in a right manner, then the relationship progresses to a higher level. If the relationship is already at level one, then it deepens and becomes more mature and solid.

> *The level of the relationship will be determined by the way those involved respond to the conflict.*

Permit conflict to be your friend in a relationship, not your enemy. Whether the relationship be in a marriage, the family, business, church, or a friendship, allow the conflict as means to deepen the relationship. Respond correctly. Choose meaningful relationships in your life.

Various Relationships

There are various relationships which we all will experience in life. Look briefly at some of these with me.

Marriage

The highest relationship in life outside a personal relationship with Jesus Christ is marriage. If a marriage relationship does not grow, then it will end. Certainly before marriage takes place, the relationship between a man and a woman needs to be a solid level one relationship. Through the experiences of life, as conflict enters the lives of a married couple, they must embrace it with a kiss and grow from it. If they do this as a couple, their marriage will become stronger. If they do not, it will diminish into a problem relationship that could conclude in divorce.

Parental

The most challenging job in the world is the job of a parent. As parents, we must seek a level one relationship with our children, one that is long-term, trusting, confidential, nonreactionary, and full of real love. Our goal should be that our children can tell us anything, because they know we will listen to them carefully in order to build this relationship.

Family

Relationships with various extended family members will exist on different levels. Many times this is determined by distance and time. Sadly, since our society is so mobile, family relationships are sometimes only surface and structured, rather than secure and solid.

Business Associates

The people with whom we work are very important people in our lives. Even though there will be various levels in these relationships, we need to show the greatest respect for each business associate. Few of these relationships will ever turn into a level one relationship, but if and when they do, we need to be grateful to God that we can still work objectively together and remain friends who love one another through the various conflicts that will occur on the job.

Church

Whether it happens in a small group Bible study or through a worship service, many levels of relationships will exist in the church. My desire for my church's members is that they know five or six people with whom they can share a level two relationship. This will usually keep them involved in the ministry of the church. If they never reach this pinnacle, then they will basically be sitters and soakers rather than ministers, and they are the ones that shy away from the church at the first sign of conflict.

Through the church, we can meet people and move into meaningful relationships. I believe it is here that you will develop most of your level one relationships in life. Why is this so? Because of the greatest commonality of all—our shared experience with God's love which covers a multitude of sins.

Friendship

Various levels of friendship will exist throughout your life. If you could reach the end of your life with five level one relationships, then you should consider yourself very blessed. Friends can be forever when Jesus Christ is involved, not only on this earth, but for all eternity in heaven.

An Evaluation of Jesus' Relationships

When you evaluate the various relationships that Jesus Christ had while He was on this earth, you learn a great deal about relationships. In fact, I believe He had relationships on four levels.

Consider the "multitude" as the level four relationships in the life of Jesus. The multitude consisted of the crowds of people who were intrigued with His life and actions. These relationships were surface relationships.

The religious people who were interested in Jesus' teachings represent the structured relationships in Jesus' life. These were the people that did not necessarily agree with Him, but heard Him speak on the hillside and in the synagogues. They were interested in religious things; therefore, what Jesus said was of special interest to them.

The secure relationships in Jesus' life, the level two relationships, were His relationships with the disciples, the twelve men who spent the greatest amount of time with Him. They traveled with Him, shared with Him, walked through various trials with Him, and trusted Him. Jesus reciprocated as He poured His life into these twelve men for three years. They built strong and secure relationships with one another. Obviously, when Judas' betrayal of Him occurred, the relationship diminished between him and Jesus as well as with the other disciples.

Jesus had other relationships in His life. He had a level one relationship with His mother, Mary. She was at the foot of the cross when He died. He also had a solid relationship with His friends Mary, Martha, and Lazarus. He was regularly in their home to spend time with them. Among the disciples, there were three men who were known as the inner circle. Peter, James, and John were very close to Jesus. They accompanied Him in the times of His greatest need and greatest glory. Each of these people shared with Him a long-term relationship, filled with trust and love.

We learn from the life of Jesus that not everyone will be your best friend nor should you expect to be everyone's best friend. Various levels of relationships are healthy for each of us, as they were for Him.

Developing Meaningful Relationships

I believe the Book of Proverbs affirms the words I have shared in this chapter when it says, "A man of many friends comes to ruin, but there is a friend who sticks closer than a brother" (Prov. 18:24). The person who thinks he has countless friends and who thinks he is a friend to great numbers of people is mistaken. In fact, Proverbs says that this leads to ruin. The passage affirms that there is a friend who sticks closer than a brother, a person with whom you have an absolutely solid relationship. This friend could be a reference to God Himself, but it is also referring to those special friends in life who are most meaningful to us.

Each relationship is either a replenishing relationship or a depleting relationship.

We know that Jesus Christ is the absolute greatest friend we can ever have in life. He never disappoints. The Bible says in John 15:13–14, "Greater love has no one than this, that one lay down his life for his friends. You are my friends, if you do what I command you." Jesus laid down His life for us. When we obey His commandments in our lives, we prove ourselves His friends. Without a doubt, He is the greatest example of that friend that sticks closer than a brother.

Each relationship is either a replenishing relationship or a depleting relationship. A replenishing relationship exists when a person fills you emotionally and spiritually, brings you life and vitality, and fills you with enthusiasm. It is someone you enjoy being with and who makes you better by being with him.

A depleting relationship exists when a person drains you emotionally and spiritually. They are more of a chore to be around than a joy. They are the people who sap your strength rather than recharge your energy. Without a doubt, these people usually come into your life when you do not need them. You may already be low spiritually and emotionally, and then their arrival contributes to your problem rather than solving it.

Every time I think about replenishing and depleting relationships in my life, it challenges me to be a replenishing friend to others rather than a depleting friend. Therefore, I must be aware of whether I am draining others or filling them with encouragement. I cannot always talk with friends about my problems, but I must be willing to listen to them share about theirs. I want to be a replenishing friend to others, the kind of friend who brings life and vitality to those with whom I relate. A great choice is to be a replenishing friend.

As I attempt to develop meaningful relationships in life, I need to remember that it is a developmental process. Allow me to close this chapter by sharing with you some insights I have gained through the years in personal and pastoral relationships.

The number seven represents perfection. Even though there are no perfect relationships because we are not perfect people, I want to share with you seven qualities which develop meaningful relationships in your life.

Commitment

If you are going to have a meaningful relationship with another person, there must be a commitment from you and that person to have it so. One of the most committed relationships in the Bible was the relationship between David and Jonathan. Jonathan was a great encourager to King David. They made a commitment to one another that their relationship would be successful. It survived as great a test as any human relationship in the Scripture.

Whenever the Lord brings special people into your life who are potential level one relationships, characterized by the word *solid*, there needs to be a commitment from each person to the relationship. A one-way commitment will not result in a meaningful relationship. The relationship will never be able to reach its full potential without commitment. There almost needs to be a verbal gesture, "I want to be your friend. I am making a commitment to you that I am going to be your friend." A meaningful relationship will not develop apart from commitment.

Time

It is essential that time is regarded as important in any meaningful relationship. You cannot build a relationship with someone without spending time with them. Time is more important in a relationship on levels two to four than it is on level one. A solid relationship is still in need of time, but it is not threatened if it is temporarily impossible to be together over a short period in the relationship.

Without a doubt, my wife and I enjoy a level one relationship. It may not be perfect, but it is solid. One of the commitments we have made to one another is that we spend each Friday together. We know that time is important—uninterrupted time—when we can refresh our relationship through catching up on all the details of the week. This is a cherished time for both of us.

Time is important in developing a meaningful relationship. Do not be deceived into thinking that any relationship in your life is above the need for uninterrupted time.

Sacrifice

A meaningful relationship will not exist unless there is a willingness to sacrifice on the part of both people. Selfishness has destroyed many relationships that were on their way to becoming meaningful. Sacrifice means that you may have to give up something you value for the sake of another person or, in this case, to establish a meaningful relationship.

If a relationship is to be solid, then it must embody the willingness to sacrifice. The relationship should be valued more than personal goals in life. Be willing to sacrifice even the valued things in life in order to cherish a meaningful relationship.

Sharing

Sharing is an ingredient of any meaningful relationship. This sharing is not only verbal sharing, but at times needs to involve the sharing of a gift. A grave danger to a relationship is to take the other person for granted. Sharing a gift with another person will demonstrate a gracious and appreciative spirit.

Sharing yourself in a relationship supersedes all other kinds of sharing. Sharing yourself with others is not easy, but it is imperative if a meaningful and solid relationship is going to exist.

Encouragement

Another insight for developing a meaningful relationship is to serve as a source of encouragement to others. Jonathan was a great encourager to David. He tried to shelter him when he was under great attack.

In a former church, a group of people whom I still do not know by name formed a Barnabas Committee. In the Book of Acts, Barnabas was a man who always encouraged others. This Barnabas Committee was anonymous. It was a group of people who determined that their role was going to be to send notes and give gifts to people to demonstrate encouragement. How this Barnabas Committee blessed my life on many occasions!

Don't you love to be around encouragers? Bless others by encouraging them. Believe me, we all need encouragement.

Trust

When commitment, time, sacrifice, sharing, and encouragement exist mutually in a relationship, trust will be established.

Without trust in a relationship, the relationship will never develop into a solid one. Trust is earned in a relationship. If trust is ever broken, it is very difficult to ever regain it.

> *Without trust in a relationship, the relationship will never develop into a solid one.*

Solid relationships are built on trust. Intimacy can only take place when trust is present in a relationship. If that trust is ever questioned, then the relationship is in for a major transition. I will trust people in a relationship until they give me reason not to do so. This approach is a positive one, rather than continually asking yourself, "I wonder if I can trust that person?" Building trust in a relationship is like building a one-mile stretch of road over water . . . it takes time.

Oneness

Oneness is the result of a developing, growing, and meaningful relationship. Hearts are only able to come together when commitment, time, sacrifice, sharing, encouragement, and trust have existed. In a marital relationship, oneness must exist. Practically, oneness can only happen when the relationship consists of the other six qualities I have mentioned.

A choice to have a meaningful relationship with someone else is not an easy choice. It is a great choice. It is a spiritual choice. It is a choice that will lead you to experience the power of God. However, choosing to have a meaningful relationship may be costly. It will cost you time, energy, and at times, some of the resources with which the Lord has blessed you.

Choose not to miss the blessing of having meaningful relationships. Every one of us needs friends like the Thompsons I mentioned in an earlier chapter or the Perkinses I shared about in this chapter. These kinds of solid relationships take work. Remember, they began because a wise and godly choice was made. We wanted to have a meaningful relationship with one another. These meaningful relationships were only able to remain solid as we continued to make the right choices in them, choices of commitment, time, sacrifice, sharing, encouragement, trust, and oneness. Choices like these will always empower me with God's power. Therefore, choosing to have meaningful relationships is always a wise choice.

❧

THIRTEEN

Choosing God's Best for Your Child

Some would think that pastoring a growing church would be the greatest challenge in my life. It is a tremendous task, but lags behind the challenge of being a father to my boys. Josh and Nicholas are the most special people in the lives of Ronnie and Jeana Floyd. Without a doubt, they are loved by their parents as much as any children could possibly be.

Even though Josh and Nicholas' grandparents believe they are perfect, their mother and I are aware that they are not. Just as they are growing in the role of being our children, we join them in the process of growing as their parents. One of the real problems with parenting is that you have the learn it "on the job." This is not always easy. How nice it would be to find all the answers in a book and pull them out when you need them. However, this is not the way it works.

More than anything else in this world, I want God's best for Josh and Nicholas. Please understand, I did not say I wanted their idea of best, but God's best for their lives. This is where parents make many grave mistakes with their children. We cannot contribute to their selfish will and desires, but we must join the Lord in bending and molding their wills so they will desire God's best. As a parent, I often think about what would be God's best for Josh and Nicholas. In my heart, I believe I know, at least in part, what that is.

God's best for their lives is for them to love Jesus and His church more than anything else in this world. When people ask me, "Pastor, how can I pray for you?" I always respond, "Pray for my boys to grow up loving Jesus and His church." As children of a pastor, they are under immense pressure. The older they get, the more they feel this pressure.

Jeana and I are committed to never making decisions on the basis of who I am as a Christian leader, but based upon who our children are under the Lord. Jeana's father was a pastor; therefore, she can identify with our boys in this sense and always keeps their welfare in the forefront of any decision we must make as a family. By the way, we do not make any big deal about who they are as the children of the pastor, nor do we tolerate jokes about them being "preacher's kids."

We are fully aware that Satan will do all he can to destroy Josh and Nicholas. This is why we do not take lightly our job as parents. Parents must be willing to fight Satan for their children. In life and in prayer, I daily tell the adversary that I refuse to give my children over to him. When our children leave us for an activity or a night away with a friend, we remind them not of who they are, but to whom they belong—Jesus.

I want my children to grow up loving Jesus and His church. What a tribute to God and to the ministry to which He has called me, to see my children live out before others the standards God has established. May God bring this about for Josh and Nicholas for His honor and glory.

When I think of God's best for Josh and Nicholas, I am led to encourage them to a life of purity and holiness. Purity and holiness are so important in our day since the attacks of Satan are so great against young people in these areas. Society does nothing to lead children to purity and holiness, but continually distracts them from it.

On the morning Josh turned thirteen years old, I challenged him to a life of moral purity by saving himself sexually for his wife. As I shared with him God's will in this area, I also gave him a gift. The gift was a gold necklace with an eagle on it. I told him that the gold symbolized purity. God's will for his life was moral purity. I shared with him that the significance of the eagle came from

> *Society does nothing to lead children to purity and holiness, but continually distracts them from it.*

Isaiah 40:31. "Yet those who wait for the Lord will gain new strength; they will mount up with wings like eagles, they will run and not get tired, they will walk and not become weary."

I told him that the eagle was to symbolize waiting until he was married to participate in sexual intercourse. I challenged him with the knowledge that he will not soar like an eagle unless he obeys God's laws in his life.

I finalized our time that morning by asking him to place the chain around his neck only if he was going to make the commitment to God, himself, and me that he would remain morally pure and save himself sexually for his wife. He placed the necklace around his neck, and then each of us prayed a prayer of commitment to God. When we concluded this prayer, I told him that the necklace would be a reminder every day of his commitment to purity. Finally, I told him that on his wedding night, I wanted him to present this necklace to his wife, telling her of its meaning—that he had saved himself sexually just for her.

I believe this is God's best for Josh and Nicholas. I will lead Nicholas in a similar experience on his thirteenth birthday.

I believe God's best for my boys is to marry a godly woman who is committed to Jesus Christ and His church. Without a doubt, this is God's will for every believer in Him. A believer should never unite in marriage with an unbeliever. This is not God's will under any condition. There is no such thing as missionary dating and marriage.

I am convinced that God's best for my boys is to have a successful career. I do not have any idea what that career is to be. This will be determined by the Lord as they individually discern it for their lives. As I pray for them daily, I am already praying for their future spouses and their career successes. I believe the Lord will honor our prayers for our children.

I believe it is God's best for Josh and Nicholas to enjoy life. I do not mean enjoy life by compromising the Word of God and joining in the ways of the world, but I mean for them to enjoy life out of their relationship to Jesus Christ. I do not believe God wants Satan to trick them into the false things of this world. I believe that true joy comes from the Lord. Recreation and career success cannot give lasting joy, but a vital relationship with Jesus Christ can.

I am aware that even as I desire the best for my children, I know that God desires it even more since they are His children. His name is more important than my name. He wants my children to be a testimony to Him.

Choosing God's best for your child is one of the highest choices in your life. What a choice of worship we make when we choose God's best for our children. A choice for God's best in your child's life is a wise and right choice.

It is a known fact that one of the major problems in our culture is the lack of proper parenting taking place in the home. Many children in our culture are not raised by their biological parents. Divorce is causing catastrophic complications in our society. Single parents have a tremendous challenge to be both mother and father to their children. Every-other-weekend parenting just does not cut it. The absence of fathers in the home has created immense insecurity that results in all types of extreme behaviors in the lives of children.

Due to a parenting problem, much of the youth culture today is involved in things that do not honor the Lord. Drugs and alcohol continue to be major problems. Guns and gangs are dominating our society. Sexual immorality is promoted through free condom distribution in many of our schools. Society is in trouble because of poor parenting rather than because of rude, immature young people. The young generation generally mirrors the morals and values of those who have been their models in life.

The desire of any parent should be for their children to experience God's best for their lives. Scripture should determine God's best for them. It is not important what I think is best unless it harmonizes with God's Word.

God's Best for Your Child

What is God's best for your child? Jesus expressed it simply. The Pharisees were the religious leaders of Jesus' day. They were always trying to test Jesus by questioning His teachings. According to the Bible, they attempted to do this in Matthew 22:36–40, asking,

> Teacher, which is the greatest commandment in the Law? And He said to them, "You shall love the Lord your God with all your heart, and with all your soul, and with all your mind." This is the great and foremost commandment. And a second is like it, "You shall love your neighbor as yourself." On these two commandments depend the whole Law and the Prophets.

Jesus taught that all of the laws of God hang on these two commandments. Therefore, if the entire counsel of God is reduced to these two commandments, then they serve as God's best for our children.

Commandment One: Love God

Loving God is the greatest spiritual act of worship we can do with our lives. Therefore, our children should be taught to love God. The Scripture says that we are to love and adore the Lord our God with all that we are in life. Jesus said you are to love God with all your heart, with all your soul, and with all your mind. What more is there in your life than your heart, soul, and mind? With our whole being, we are to love God. This is God's will for us. This is God's best for your child.

> God's best for my child is not to love the things of this world . . . but to love Him.

Do you believe God's best for your child is to love Him? We cannot be deceived by Satan and drawn into the insignificant things of life. God's best for my child is not to love the things of this world, or to love the applause of this world, or to love the acceptance of this world, but to love Him. As a parent, I must not be found guilty of teaching my children to love everything else above God. He is Lord. He is God. He deserves our love. This is God's best for you and me. This is God's best for your child. Choose God's best for your child by training him to love God.

Commandment Two: Love Others

Without a doubt, we are to love others even as we love ourselves. I believe that Jesus taught us that we cannot love others until we first love ourselves. I have observed for years that when people cannot love others, it is because they do not love themselves. Jesus affirms that we are to love others as He loves them. He loves them unconditionally, sacrificially, and willfully.

God's best for your child is to love other people. They learn this early in life. If selfishness and tempers are permitted when they are young, then eventually they will not be able to express love to others. At times, we laugh at the little disagreements and fights between children. Yet they really need to be taught early that loving others is second to loving God. Disrespect toward other children, adults, and parents should never be tolerated. God's best for your child is to love others.

The most important love relationship we have in life is toward God. This is a vertical relationship. The second most important love relationship we have is with other people. These are horizontal relationships. I have seen for years that if the vertical relationship of loving God is not what it needs to be, then horizontal relationships with others will not be what they should be. Therefore, when we struggle to love others, it is because our relationship with Jesus is not one of loving Him with our all.

Choose God's best for your child by training your child to love others the way Jesus loves them. Remember, He loves all people unconditionally, sacrifically, and willfully.

These two commandments are the greatest two things we can teach our children—all else is secondary. Loving God and others is God's best for them. Choose to train your children in each of these spiritual exercises. It will make them strong and mighty for God. It will enable their lives to be filled with meaningful relationships. This is a great choice for you.

As parents, we need to make wise choices in relationship to our children based on God's Word. Loving God and others is a choice for spiritual power. As a parent, how are you responsible for choosing the things that are God's best for your children?

Parental Responsibilities

Everything that happens to your child cannot be laid at your feet as a parent. We can do only so much; however, are we doing everything that we need to be doing? We cannot throw our hands up and say, "I have done what I can do . . . the rest is up to him." We are responsible for our children. We cannot disregard our God-ordained responsibilities. At the same time, we should not live in guilt for our entire lives if our children grow up making bad choices. The key is that we have made right choices for them as long as we have been able to influence them.

As a pastor, I am convinced that many of the younger generation's problems today can be traced back to parents. It seems that the goal of some parents is to be popular with their child. They cannot bear the thought of not having their child's approval. With such a goal, many parents cease being the leaders of their children and simply follow the desires of the children. In the mind of a parent, this eases tension in the home and helps their child to like them a little more. But a godly parent should not live with the desire to become popular with his children, but rather to be respected by them. This will only come as parents know what is right under God and with a gentle spirit lead their children to doing what God wants them to do in life.

I want to condense the responsibilities of parents into three specific areas. Please remember, God's best for your child is to love Him and to love others. Therefore, since these serve as our goals, how are we responsible for our children and accountable to God for them?

Lead Them by Integrity

The integrity crisis in America, discussed earlier in this book, is not isolated to leadership in government, church, and business. There is an integrity crisis in the home. This crisis is with parents who do not lead their children. We cannot empower our children to greatness by telling them one thing and living another. We must lead them by integrity.

> We cannot empower our children to greatness by telling them one thing and living another.

The Bible speaks about parents leading their children with integrity in Proverbs 20:7: "A righteous man who walks in his integrity—how blessed are his sons after him."

A parent who walks in integrity models what is right before his children. The child will not only be told what is right for his life, but he will see what is right lived out through the lives of his parents. Righteousness may be more caught than taught. The proverb affirms that the sons of a man who walks in integrity will be blessed. In fact, there is an indication that the sons will follow in the same way as their father.

What an awesome responsibility it is for a parent to lead their children with integrity. If we want our children to live righteously, then they must see it before their eyes while they are under the influence of their parents. As our choices follow our convictions based on God's Word, our children will witness real integrity. Perhaps when they are tempted in their lives to compromise, they will remember the courage of their parents and choose integrity. Choose to lead your children with integrity.

Train Them in Godliness

Whenever we read from the Proverbs we need to follow correct interpretive principles in regard to biblical hermeneutics. A proverb is a general truth brought to bear on a specific situation. A proverb is not an absolute guarantee.

We need to remember this whenever we read the Proverbs. This is especially true when we come to various passages which people hold on to with hope and promise. One of these is found in Proverbs 22:6: "Train up a child in the way he should go, even when he is old he will not depart from it."

As we interpret this Scripture, we need to know that this is a general principle for parents and children; however, it is not an absolute guarantee that our children will never leave the path God has planned for them.

There may be situations in which a parent has done exactly what they should in training their child. Yet the powerful and selfish will of the child was never mastered, and he lives a life filled with bad choices. As a parent, if you have been obedient in your training of that child, the training will never depart from them. No matter how far they walk from the godly standard set for them, they are aware of their waywardness from that standard.

I want to come back to this Scripture, but let me share a word with parents who have children who have fallen away from the faith. Remember, God is the perfect Father to us, but there are many times we have fallen away from Him. This does not reflect on God as a poor Father, but on us and on our selfishness that has resulted in some bad choices in our lives.

You may have been an excellent parent, but each child must finally determine in which direction they are going in their lives. We can train them to make right choices, but in the trenches of life, they must make their own choices. Never lose faith in what God may still do in their lives. Release them to the Lord for Him to deal with them.

Since Proverbs 22:6 is such an important verse for parents and children, I want us to return there for explanation. Training children in this text means putting something into their mouth to affect their taste. It also means to dedicate, set aside, or start your child by narrowing his conduct in a proper way. This proverb encourages the parent to take advantage of early training in a child's life by pointing him toward godliness. The warning that is given to parents is that a child should not have his own way while he is young or else as he grows older, even into adulthood, he will choose a self-willed lifestyle. The way a child should be trained to go is God's way, not his own. Therefore, if God's way is not his choice while he is young, discipline needs to be exercised.

If a child's life is influenced to go God's way, his early training will probably lead him never to depart from the godliness he was taught in his youthful life. If we start them right, the chances are, they will finish right. Right in this case is godliness—God's way.

I really believe the heart of everything that I have written in this chapter can be discovered in Deuteronomy 6:5–9,

> And you shall love the Lord your God with all your heart and with all your soul and with all your might. And these words, which I am commanding you today, shall be on your

heart; and you shall teach them diligently to your sons and shall talk of them when you sit in your house and when you walk by the way and when you lie down and when you rise up. And you shall bind them as a sign on your hand and they shall be as frontals on your forehead. And you shall write them on the doorposts of your house and on your gates.

This verse gives the main goal for our children—to love God with their all. In every situation in life, from morning to night, we must train them to love God. They must see it modeled before them through the lives of their parents. Even our houses should be a testimony that we love God with all that we are and all that we have in this life. Consistency and persistency should forever train them in godliness.

The challenge is to accept responsibility as parents to train your children, to influence their lives with your godliness.

When this is our life message to our children, they will be more likely never to depart from it. The challenge is to accept responsibility as parents to train your children, to influence their lives with your godliness. The church or a Christian school is not commissioned to do these tasks for you. Choose a church and a school that support the godly principles you are teaching your children at home. If these institutions do not support the instruction that you are attempting to give them in your home, then find ones that will. But do not abdicate your role as primary teacher and model to your church or your children's school.

One of the reasons I am a firm believer in quality, excellent, well-balanced Christian education for children is that they need the godliness taught in the home reaffirmed in their school. They are under a mighty influence from morning till mid-afternoon five days a week for nine months each year. If that influence is not reaffirming what I am teaching at home, then I am fighting a difficult battle. I will not gamble on whether my boys can handle that or not. I am talking about their souls, their strength, their minds, and their futures.

Many argue against Christian schools for Christian children, insisting they need to be lights in their worlds. I agree with that fully; however, the proper church and the proper home can help affirm the need for them to be witnesses to a world without Christ. An educated, secular-minded teacher is able to intimidate any child so that his views dominate the godly convictions of a child. I want my children influenced with godliness from morning until evening.

Thank God for the Christian teachers and administrators who have stayed in the battle for quality public education. Without them, it would already be totally atheistic in philosophy. We need to pray for Christian teachers and administrators that they will be willing and able to stand for what is right and teach with courage, regardless of what the system says to do.

We need to pray for the children of our nation who have no choice in where they attend school. Their parents may be unable to send them to a quality Christian school or there may not be one where they live. I believe the government needs to give parents the choice of where they educate their children. By providing vouchers, parents would be free to choose where their children are educated without government intervention. Some think this would be the demise of the public school system. I believe, to the contrary, that it may be the only hope for the public school system. This monopoly needs to be broken and we should allow competition to exist. This would force the public education system, the private schools, and the Christian schools of this country to provide quality education in every area. Even at this, Christian parents must choose schools for their children that will support the godly values and principles they are being taught at home or they are gambling with the future of their children. Our responsibility is to train our children in godliness from the time they get up in the morning until the time they go to bed at night.

Discipline Them with Love

There are many verses in the Bible about disciplining your child. I want to highlight just one. "Discipline your son while there is hope, and do not desire his death" (Prov. 19:18).

Interesting, isn't it—hope in your child's life is dependent on your discipline. A parent who is not willing to perform discipline is missing the window of opportunity God gives them to influence that young life to be godly.

Discipline is the process that keeps your child walking in the lane of godliness. As you set the biblical boundaries for your child and he lives within them, he experiences freedom in his life. If you child steps outside the boundaries, it is your responsibility as the parent to bring correction to the child. Failure to discipline your child leads him to a life of bad choices governed only by self-will. It takes courage to practice correction of your children. To love your child is to discipline him when he makes selfish or un-Christlike choices. Disciplining your child is an act of love. It is not easy, but it is necessary.

As parents lead their children with integrity, train them in godliness, and discipline them with love, they are acting as responsible parents. These serve as God's ways to teach your child to love Him and to love others. This is God's best for your child.

Choosing God's Best for Your Child

What is the most effective way you can choose God's best for your child? In the final section of this chapter, I want to offer some practical insights about how you can choose God's best as a parent.

Model Godliness

One of the greatest ways a parent can choose God's best for their child is to model godliness before them. There needs to be complete harmony in what we say and what we do before our children. Integrity calls us to model godliness before them.

Children like having heroes. In our society, many of these heroes may be superb in athletics or music. However, most of them do not serve as the Christian role models we want our children to emulate. Parents can become role models who gain the respect of children. Just know that children really do not appreciate their parents as models of godliness until they are moving from adolescence to adulthood. We model godliness consistently before them, believing one day in the future our children will embrace us with admiration and respect.

Pray with Your Child

One of the most effective ways to choose God's best for your child is not only to pray *for* them daily, but to pray *with* them. Children need to hear their parents intercede for them before the Lord. They need to hear their parents asking God to guide them and supply their needs.

God's best for your child is not only to pray for them daily, but to pray with them.

I am asked often, "What should be done in family devotions?" I believe there are many ways family devotions can be done, but let me share with you what we have found to be effective in our family. I do not believe a daily family devotion needs to consist of a thirty minute Bible study coupled with a thirty minute prayer meeting. I believe if you will teach your children through life situations, they gain more value from spiritual principles taught in this way so that family devotions are consistent with who you are and what you teach all day long.

If you can consistently meet with your family at least five days a week for special prayer and on some days give them a word from the Bible, you will accomplish the purpose of a family devotional time. With family schedules so haphazard, I strongly suggest that you begin your day with a devotional time before everyone leaves to go their separate ways. This will also be a time when you touch base with one another and encourage one another to have an enjoyable day in the Lord.

Participate with Your Child

Parents can choose God's best for their child when they participate in their children's activities. Whether it is a ballgame, gymnastics, recital, or some other special interest in their lives, parents need to participate in these activities with their children. This demonstrates to them that they are important to you. I will change schedules and have even canceled engagements to participate in something that is important to my children.

In the summer of 1993, Josh played in the Babe Ruth World Series. I had the choice of being in Sunday evening worship or being at that crucial game. I chose to be at his game. If it had been a regular season game, he would not have played on Sunday nor would I have participated in it. However, we had already honored the Lord that morning by attending worship and Bible study. Therefore, I chose to miss our evening worship service to be at the World Series ball game. I received no criticism for that action. In fact, when it was announced where the pastor was, the people applauded. I modeled before my people the importance of my children in my life. A sermon could not have said it as well as that choice did.

Trust Your Child

One of the most incredible challenges for a parent is learning to release your child. As you permit them to venture from your protection, trust is needed. Trusting them involves building a personal relationship with them.

I believe you should trust your children until they give you reason not to do so. When this happens, then it is time to teach them through using their particular life situation to learn a spiritual principle.

Every Christian parent should desire God's best for their children. This goal of loving God and loving others demands we be responsible parents, the kind of parents that lead with integrity, train in godliness, and discipline with love. When we choose to be responsible parents, we must model godliness. Pray with them, participate in what is important to them, and trust them enough to build a meaningful relationship with them.

A choice to see God's best come into your child's life is a choice to have a meaningful relationship. It is a choice to experience God's power in your life. As you experience this power, your child will be influenced to choose God's best for their life.

❧

FOURTEEN

Choosing What Is Right for the Next Generation

Of the approximately 250 million people living in America, 77.5 percent of them live in metropolitan areas.[1] No longer are we a rural nation. The challenges are numerous for the vast percentage of the population living in our cities. Homelessness and an alarming rise in violent crime are but two of the monumental problems which plague our nation's cities.

America is a complex nation. Statistics as compiled by the *U.S. Almanac* profile the demographics of our population:

➤ 25.8% of the population is under 18 years of age

➤ 12.6% of the population is 65 years of age or older

➤ $19,092 is the per capita income

➤ 14.2% of the population falls below the poverty line per year

➤ 14.0% of the population is not covered by health insurance

➤ $4,114 federal taxes are paid per person per year

➤ $5,482 is the public school spending per student per year
➤ 71.2% of the population has graduated from high school
➤ 758.1 violent crimes are committed per 100,000 people per year[2]

In addition, one-fourth of the population of America is nonwhite or Hispanic. This figure is expected to be one-third by the year 2030.[3]

These statistics bring to our attention the challenges facing our nation today and in the future. There are many potential problems contained in these demographic facts, and they will have a major impact on the next generation of Americans—their future will be affected greatly.

When we consider that over one quarter (25.8%) of the country's total population is under eighteen years of age, we can only imagine the challenge this poses for our society in the future. Families, churches, schools, and businesses cannot ignore this great segment of our population. Their needs are many and diverse. The changing times in American family life have compounded the already difficult experience of growing up for many children and teenagers.

Conversely, America is also an aging nation. With 12.6 percent of the population being sixty-five years of age or older, we are confronted with problems that have not been around before. The technological advancements in the field of medicine coupled with a growing emphasis on health and diet have resulted in people living longer. Who will care for the aged in our country? With health care costs rising dramatically, there is a financial impact on families today as never before. The children of aging parents are now faced with determining how to care for loved ones in order to make the final years of their lives productive and meaningful. How we care for the elderly also makes a strong impression on our young people.

Poverty is a growing reality in America. What can be done about the poverty in ours, the wealthiest of nations? What will the next generation do about it? Government resources are increasingly limited. The problem of poverty contributes to a myriad of other problems such as abortion, illegitimate births, hunger, crime, and lack of adequate health care.

Always known as the "great melting pot," we find our society struggling to accommodate the increasing numbers immigrating from other countries in search of liberty, freedom, and prosperity. The challenge is great as we attempt to deal with the many demands this situation creates. How will we care for their needs in literacy and healthcare? It is not an impossible task, but tremendously challenging. The next generation must be creative if it is to meet these pressing and growing needs.

Since so many of these problems will be felt most acutely by members of the next generation, we need to prepare and equip them the best we can. I do not know of a greater challenge for the church today than investing time, energy, and money in the young people of this country. We have an opportunity through the church to teach these children and young people spiritual principles which can enable them to be responsible citizens.

We are not leaving a healthy and strong nation for them to inherit. We are leaving them a nation seriously lacking direction and positive influence, a nation that is no longer a strong advocate of moral absolutes, but one that determines what is right based upon circumstance.

Our choices have determined the present status and will determine the future of America. We have made poor choices in regard to God. He is no longer regarded with reverence by our citizens. He is ridiculed by various groups who have made it their agenda to remove religious influence from our nation.

We have made poor choices in regard to life. We kill the unborn and permit the death of those who do not desire to live any more.

We have eliminated prayer in our public schools. The choice of our nation to wink at the perversion of human sexuality in the forms of adultery and homosexuality, which are strictly forbidden in Holy Scripture, brings a terrible and destructive legacy for the next generation.

We are sending the wrong signals to our young people because of our un-Christlike choices which are in total opposi-tion to the Bible. Small wonder that there is such confusion in the minds of our children. The signals we are sending them are ambiguous, compounding their confusion. We are not only leaving them with a multitude of problems, but worse still, we are not leaving them with the kind of convictions which will en-able them to grapple successfully with those problems to insure that America remains a great nation.

> *We are sending the wrong signals to our young people because of our un-Christlike choices which are in total opposition to the Bible.*

The problems are great. The challenges are many. Change is certain. What are the major crises facing the next generation?

Crises Facing the Next Generation

Even though I have mentioned some of the problems facing the next generation, I want to highlight three of them in this chapter. I do not believe they are insignificant problems but major crises facing the next generation.

Moral Crisis

Humanism has been a destructive force to the moral fiber of America. The morality built upon Judeo-Christian ethics has been viciously attacked in our country. Humanism places man as the center of everything and results in secularism which pushes God out of everything. We get morality from God, not from ourselves. Since we are sinful by nature, morality can only come from God. The principles and ethics upon which this nation was built are now treated like outdated relics on a museum shelf.

Humanism promotes the heretical teaching that there are no moral absolutes in life—no right and wrong. Do what you feel, what is right in your own eyes. Humanism changes the laws of the land to ease the punishment when a flagrant act such as murder is permitted. Humanism scoffs at capital punishment and exalts human civil liberties above justice. Since there is no right or wrong in the eyes of the humanist, they are hard pressed to deal with those who commit flagrant, violent acts which harm others.

Because humanism has been so palatable to decision makers in government and education, we have now raised millions of people who ascribe to this great lie. The result is that the future of the next generation is in jeopardy because of the amoral beliefs that exist in this nation. What a tragic picture of America!

The amoral attitude of our nation now permits the killing of at least 1.5 million babies each year by abortion.[4] The factors determining whether one gets an abortion today are convenience and affordability rather than what is morally right. The leadership of our nation is concerned about the growing problem of child abuse, but has little concern about killing the unborn. What a contradiction! Without a doubt, the most dangerous place for a child to live today is in his or her mother's womb.

The amoral beliefs pervading our nation advocate expanding the concept of human sexuality to include the practices of homosexuality. Many in the next generation are being raised in households of men living with men or women living with women who practice immoral sexual behavior.

The homosexual community is crying loudly, seeking recognition and treatment as a legitimate minority group. They want to hold jobs in which they have direct supervision of and influence upon young people. The present administration has appointed homosexuals to high positions of authority in the White House, and it takes every opportunity to reassure us that it considers this lifestyle to be acceptable.

Bear in mind, it was the practice of homosexuality that brought destruction upon Sodom and Gomorrah in the Old Testament. As I have heard said on many occasions, "If God does not judge America for this sin, He will have to apologize to Sodom and Gomorrah."

The amoral mentality by which many have chosen to live in America will also leave the next generation monumental problems in the area of crime. Drive-by shootings are not only happening in major cities but all over the country. Gangs outnumber policemen in some cities. Guns are now taken to school by mere children. As a result, teachers, administrators and other children are being murdered. People are now walking into restaurants and other places of business and opening fire on innocent people with little or no provocation.

We are living in a nation that is infected with crime. An amoral mentality has contributed greatly to the alarming deterioration of the value system of our country.

The belief that there are no absolutes, no right or wrong, is now destroying the educational institutions in America. The curriculum taught in the classrooms propagates this error. Decisions are being made based on this mentality that will affect the next generation. Tragedy will continue if we do not see a change in the teaching of our children regarding right and wrong.

The moral crisis in our country is a terrible burden to place on our children. But our nation's choices will plague the future generations for their entire lives and beyond, unless some miracle occurs. Sadly, the moral crisis is not the only one they will face.

Economic Crisis

America is in economic trouble. We are short-sighted, committed to the short-term solution rather than what is best for the long-term for the economy of our country.

We are leaving the next generation trillions of dollars in debt. They may never have it as good as we have had it in our lives economically. Many believe that America will one day experience total bankruptcy as a nation. I am not certain about our economic future, but I am certain that it is another great burden soon to fall on the shoulders of the next generation.

One example of our nation's failure to address its problems is in the area of the rising cost of health care. A socialist approach to medicine is being strongly considered. The government cannot possibly meet all the needs in our nation. Yet, doesn't everyone deserve the right to be cared for physically? Who will pay for it? The provision of health care is just one of many challenges which will be left to our children.

Spiritual Crisis

I believe every crisis that America is experiencing and will experience in the future is rooted in a spiritual crisis the worst crisis of all. Due to this spiritual crisis, humanism and secularism have gained immense popularity.

Vast number of churches in America have plateaued or are declining in membership. Tradition seems to be more important than reaching the present generation. The authority of the Bible is not even accepted by many of these churches. Evangelism and ministry are no longer passions, but are regarded as antiquated, needless, and burdensome.

The spiritual crisis exists in our nation because of the spiritual crisis in the pulpits of America. Where are the passionate preachers of the gospel of Jesus Christ? Where are the dynamic, Spirit-anointed preachers, who are full of vision and drive to see America experience a spiritual revival? Where are the prophets of America, courageous enough to denounce amoral and immoral behaviors and to pronounce boldly what is right in the sight of God?

This spiritual crisis should not be transferred to the next generation. Together we need to deal with our spiritual problems and seek the correct spiritual solutions to them. Then there will be hope for the next generation.

Hope for the Next Generation

Although they face what seems to be insurmountable crises, there is hope for the next generation. The Bible says in Proverbs 14:34, "Righteousness exalts a nation, but sin is a disgrace to any people." This verse presents some interesting truths for the present and next generation of this country. It gives us the reason for hopelessness and the reason for hope.

The Reason for Hopelessness

The word *sin* is used in contrast to righteousness. Hopelessness is the result of a nation that ignores sin.

As long as America ignores its sin problem, our future is hopeless. Whether the sin is a societal one of abortion, homosexuality, crime, or personal one of a critical spirit, lust, or greed, the result is the same—hopelessness. When sin abounds in a nation, that nation will be disgraced.

The Reason for Hope

Even though it seems hopeless for our nation and the next generation, there is reason to hope. My hope is in the Lord God Almighty, not in politics or people. The proverb just cited teaches that when we make the right choices—the kind of choices that lead us to righteousness—the Lord will exalt our nation.

I believe the future of our nation is in making right choices. A profound difference could be made if God's people would choose righteousness rather than sin. The Lord promises that we will be lifted up out of our sin if we will choose righteousness.

I believe across America today there is a growing concern for the next generation. We are beginning to question what we are going to leave them. I do not believe that many in our country feel good about the legacy we are creating.

Therefore, now is the time to promote hope to our nation. Now is the time to choose righteousness. This will place hope in our hearts, hope for the present and for the future of America.

We owe it to the next generation to make good and godly choices toward righteousness. What are some of the choices that will truly assist the next generation?

Choices that Will Assist the Next Generation

I believe there are many choices which could be helpful, but there are five choices that each of us needs to make daily for hope and peace to fill America's people.

Affirm the Bible as the Word of God

The first choice we need to make daily is to affirm that the Bible is the Holy Word of God. It does not simply contain the Word of God, but it is the Word of God. It is to be our authority for all of life. The Bible is the perfect treasure of God. Whenever it speaks, it is authoritative and indisputable.

If [the next generation] chooses to continue in the same vein as the present generation, then the America we know will no longer exist.

Society needs an authoritative source for living. In the past, when the Bible was that source, the nation was exalted. Now the Bible is ridiculed, mocked, and degraded. Look around to see the results. It is our refusal to allow His authority in our lives that has placed us in the crisis we are experiencing in our nation today.

Churches, families, schools, and government need to affirm the Bible as the Word of God. It is full of clear teachings and wise counsel on how to make right choices in life. We must return to what is right.

The future of the members of the next generation will depend on whether they affirm the Bible as the Word of God. If they choose to continue in the same vein as the present generation, then destruction will accelerate, and in a matter of time, the America we know will no longer exist. The burden is on us to return now to the Bible as our source of all authority. We must transfer to our children a nation of hope and potential, not one destined for doom.

Pray for Spiritual Awakening

One of the greatest choices we can make that will assist the next generation is to pray daily for spiritual awakening. I am burdened for the spiritual condition of America. We can attack the symptoms of our problem like some of the sins we have already mentioned; however, our real problem is a spiritual one and needs to be handled in a spiritual way.

Quite honestly, my outlook would be one of doom if I did not believe in the power of prayer. Because I know the Bible is the Word of God, I believe God enables us to claim His promises through the power of prayer. I am daily asking God to bring spiritual awakening to our nation.

The church cannot stay asleep if this is to happen. It is past time to wake up. The alarm is sounding. We are just seconds away from the midnight of judgment.

God's people coming alive afresh in the Spirit is the only hope for our nation and for the next generation. We need to leave the next generation a spiritual heritage. We need to experience awakening not only for ourselves but for them. Otherwise, we will leave them dead churches that are more concerned with temporal and social issues than with the power of God to fill their lives with hope.

As God's people, we need to join in one unified chorus asking God for spiritual awakening in our country. It might seem hopeless, but it is not. Even though the times are perilous, it is in times such as these that God has brought great spiritual awakening before. Therefore, for the sake of the next generation, let us kneel before God, beseeching Him to send spiritual awakening to our land.

Focus on the Family

Dr. James Dobson's ministry, *Focus on the Family*, is doing more than any other I know to try to centralize American thought and concern around the family. As he clarifies the focus for us, we each need to begin with our own family. The family is the greatest institution today. We cannot attempt to redefine it by the sinful times in which we live. We must affirm it as God does in His Word.

The next generation does not need to inherit a warped view of the family. Even though the problems in today's families are complex, there is hope. The hope is found in returning to what God teaches in His Word about family life.

We cannot be sidetracked; God is the only One who determines what the family is to be. We cannot bend or budge on what He says about family life.

The next generation needs to receive from us a strong belief in the sanctity of the family unit. They need to receive from us lives that have been trained to focus on family living. They need to know that the greatest entity in the world today is the family. One of the only hopes for the next generation is to focus on the family.

Lift up the Standard of Moral Absolutes

We dare not be silent any longer. The next generation needs to hear from us that there are moral absolutes in our society. They need to see us lift them up far above the vain cries of the humanist and secularist philosophies. These moral absolutes will do more for their future than any of the erroneous philosophies being propagated today.

Our choices today need to reflect that we conduct our lives by these moral absolutes. These choices have the power to transfer to the next generation. This is one of their only hopes. We cannot permit muddled, unclear signals to be given anymore. It is time to let our choices lift up the standard of moral absolutes.

Disciple People from the Next Generation

Finally, a choice that will assist the next generation is to invest your life in them. You can do a great thing by discipling young people in a personal way to affirm the Bible as the Word of God, to pray for spiritual awakening, to focus on the family, and to lift up the standard of moral absolutes. When you inject these strong beliefs into their lives, you are assisting them in a mighty way.

A joy I have each month is meeting with a group of about twenty-five young people and college students in our church called "The Servants Fellowship." This group has surrendered their lives to full-time Christian service. In this meeting, I pour my life into them. I train them and disciple them in areas of personal devotion, family living, and ministry preparation. Only God knows what will eventually happen to these people, but I am fully aware that they are some of the future Christian leaders of America. They will be the hope for the next generation.

Who are you bringing alongside you from the next generation? Who are you investing your life in who is younger than twenty-five years of age? By teaching principles that will enable these young people to make the right choices in life, we can endow the next generation with hope. If I am going to have a meaningful relationship with the next generation, then I must transfer spiritual principles to them that will help them make the kind of choices to secure their future, not jeopardize it.

These five choices will assist the next generation in making right choices, choices to enable them to deal with the crises they will face in their adulthood.

With each choice you make, you should consider, "Is this a good choice for the next generation?" Our choices determine their future. Therefore, we need to make choices that demonstrate Christlikeness, that will empower the next generation with spiritual power, real success, and meaningful relationships.

F I F T E E N

Choosing Jesus

I shared with you earlier in this book how I chose Jesus Christ to be my Lord and Savior when I was fifteen years of age. I had followed religion as far as I could follow it. It only led me to hopelessness and emptiness in my life. In this search, I became aware of my deep need for a relationship with Jesus Christ.

As I was walking down the road of religion, I became aware of my sinfulness. It was obvious to me that I was in trouble spiritually. At the highest point of conviction, I became keenly aware that it was deeply sinful not to have a personal relationship with Jesus. I became aware that if I died without Him in my life, I would be separated from God forever in a place called hell.

I also became aware that there was hope for me. I knew God loved me and that He had a plan for my life. In my search to know Jesus, I realized that I could really find Him and know Him in a personal way. Sick of myself and my sin, I determined that I was ready to meet Jesus.

The greatest and most significant choice of all was when I chose Jesus Christ to be my Lord and Savior.

On a Saturday evening while attending a youth fellowship, I gave my life to Jesus Christ. I admitted to Him that I was a sinner. I acknowledged my desire to turn from my sin and receive Him into my life to be my Lord and Savior. I openly confessed to Him that I knew He died for me and was raised from the dead. I opened my heart to Jesus and received Him into my life.

On that evening, I entered into a personal relationship with Jesus Christ. I have never been the same since that night. I am not perfect and still sin, but since that day, my desire has been to follow Jesus. I have failed Him in many ways, but my desire has been to follow Him. I am a follower of Jesus Christ. I belong only to Him. I am bound for heaven when I die. I live my life now knowing that He is the Lord and Savior of my life.

The evening I chose Jesus was the greatest evening of my life. There have been other choices that have been good ones. It was a good choice for me to marry Jeana. It was a good choice for me to surrender to God's calling in my life. It was a good choice to pursue excellence through education. However, the greatest and most significant choice of all was when I chose Jesus Christ to be my Lord and Savior. This is the only eternal choice I will ever make in my life.

Choose Jesus for Eternity

This entire book has been about making the right choices in life. You may have made the right choice about a career, a spouse, a friend, and about where to live. However, not one of these choices is an eternal choice.

You can live your entire life making good choices, but if you do not make the right choice about receiving Jesus Christ into your life, you have failed to make the most important choice of all. Your other good choices will be meaningless for eternity. Religion, church membership, baptism—none of them are enough. Jesus Christ is the only way to God. The Bible says in Romans 10:13, "Whoever will call upon the name of the Lord will be saved."

The choice I am going to ask you to make right now as you complete this book is the choice to receive Jesus Christ. If you will pray the following words, or similar words, to Jesus Christ and mean them in your heart, Jesus will come into your life.

> Dear Jesus, I know I am a sinner and I do wrong every day in my life. I turn from my sin right now and open my life to Jesus Christ. I know Jesus died for me. Right now, I open my heart and say, "Jesus, come into my life." By faith, right now, I receive Jesus Christ into my life to be my Lord and Savior. Thank You for the gift of eternal life. Thank You for coming into my life. Amen.

Did you mean the words you just prayed to the Lord? If you did, Jesus Christ just became your Savior. You just made the right choice for the all eternity. Welcome to the family of God.

Choose Jesus for Today

Once you have chosen Jesus for eternity, you are equipped to make choices that will enable you to live a powerful spiritual life. For the believer in Jesus Christ, daily choices are not insignificant. Each choice is an important choice. When we make the choice to live under the lordship of Jesus Christ, we experience spiritual power, real success, and meaningful relationships in life. Your challenge every day is to live by spiritual principles that will empower your life with the Holy Spirit of God.

Choose Jesus early in the morning, and spend your entire day under His lordship. Choose to read your Bible and pray. I promise you that this will result in a spiritually powerful life.

Choose Jesus in your family. Place each member of your family under Jesus' lordship daily. Choose to place upon each of them the armor of God. Choose to love them with the kind of love Jesus has for you. Choose to provide for them not only the things of the world, but provide them the spiritual guidance they need for their lives. Choose each week to spend some time with your family in praying for specific needs for others as well as for your family.

> *There will be opportunities daily to honor Him, so take advantage of them for Jesus' sake.*

Choose Jesus in your church. He is the Head of the church. Therefore, place yourself and the entire church under His lordship. Choose to serve Jesus through your local church. Understand your spiritual gifts and use them for God's glory in your church. Choose to participate daily in the mission of your church—which should be to make disciples—by going, baptizing, and teaching them the spiritual principles that will empower their lives daily. Exalt Jesus in your church!

Choose Jesus in your job every day. He goes with you everywhere, even in the marketplace. Choose to honor Him with your conversation and your decisions. Choose to honor the Lord by working hard daily. Choose to honor the Lord by submitting to the authority over you. Honor your supervisor on the job.

Choose Jesus in every activity of your life. There will be opportunities daily to honor Him, so take advantage of them for Jesus' sake. Remember, Jesus is interested in everything you do, so choose Him daily in your life.

Wherever you go and whatever you do, choose Jesus. It is the most important choice you will ever make. If you choose Him daily, you will experience spiritual power, real success and meaningful relationships. Choosing Jesus is a choice to God's power.

Throughout this book, I have encouraged you to make choices to God's power. A Jesus choice is a powerful choice. A song that relates my challenge to you is, "I Choose Jesus." I pray that you will choose Jesus. If you do, your life will never be the same because of the choices that you will make for God's power.

I CHOOSE JESUS
(Words and Music by Robert Sterling)

Some say life is just a series of decisions.
We make choices. We live and learn.
Now I'm standing at a crossroad,
and I must choose which way to turn.

Down the one road lies all the world can offer.
All its power, its wealth and fame.
Down the other just a Man with nail scars in His hands.
But there is mercy in His eyes,
And there is power in His name.

I choose Jesus. I choose Jesus.
Without a solitary doubt, I choose Jesus.
Not for miracles, but for loving me.
Not for Bethlehem, but for Calvary.
Not for a day, but for eternity . . . I choose Jesus.

All my life I sailed the sea of reason.
I was captain of my soul.
There was no need for a Savior.
I could live life on my own.
Then I heard Him speak the language of healing
for broken lives.

When they nailed Him to a tree,
His love included me.
Now He's calling me to follow,
and leave the past behind.[1]

✧

Notes

Chapter 1
1. Corrie ten Boom with John and Elizabeth Sherrill, *The Hiding Place* (New York: Bantam Books, Inc., 1983), 197–200.
2. Dave Branon, "Pointman," *Sports Spectrum,* December 1993.
3. Ibid.
4. Ibid.

Chapter 14
1. "U.S. Almanac: Comparing State Stats," *Scholastic Update,* January 1993.
2. Ibid.
3. Ibid.
4. "The War Against the Unborn" distributed by Concerned Women for America.

Chapter 15
1. Robert Sterling, "I Choose Jesus" (Word, Inc., 1989). Used with permission.